D1355820

A Motor-Flight through France

CHAUVIGNY: RUINS OF CASTLE

EDITH WHARTON

A Motor-Flight Through France

PICADOR

First published 1908 by Macmillan & Co

This edition published 1995 by Picador
an imprint of Macmillan General Books
25 Eccleston Place London SW1W 9NF
and Basingstoke

Associated companies throughout the world

ISBN 0 330 34397 1

1 3 5 7 9 8 6 4 2

A CIP catalogue record for this book is available from
the British Library

Typeset by CentraCet Limited, Cambridge
Printed by Mackays of Chatham PLC, Chatham, Kent

Contents

Illustrations

Introduction by Julian Barnes

THE FIRST MICHELIN GUIDE TO FRANCE – limp-bound, pocket-sized, and, of course, red – came out in 1900. 'The appearance of this work', the foreword pomped, 'coincides with that of the new century, and the one will last as long as the other. The art of motoring has just been born; it will develop with each year, and the tyre will develop with it, since the tyre is the essential organ without which the car cannot travel.' The years between 1900 and 1914 were a blessed age for motorists (and, no doubt, tyre-developers): a time at which – for those who could afford it – technology seemed to have advanced the possibilities of pleasure with no apparent drawback. 'In those days,' Ford Madox Ford recalled, 'the automobile was a rapturous novelty, and when we had any buckshee money at all it went on hiring cars.' Henry James declared that 'the motor is a magical marvel', and there can have been few more attractive countries in which to turn loose its magic than what he called 'this large smooth old France.'

Edith Wharton – like Ford, like Conrad, like Kipling – took to motoring with a passion. The rapturous novelty was modern yet also cleverly historical, since it restored what Wharton describes on the first page of this book as 'the romance of travel', offering the 'recovered pleasures' experienced by 'our posting grandparents'. What had destroyed these pleasures were the iron routes and timetables of the railway;

now the motorist was freed from such dependency, and could enjoy a sharp sense of increased individual liberty. As the Baedeker Guide to Southern France of 1907 – the year in which she undertook the second of her three 'motor-flights' – candidly put it: 'Motoring enjoys an enormous vogue in France, principally owing to the absence of police-restrictions and to the excellent roads.' From the opposite end of the century, when Europe's autoroutes are clogged with freight, and individual vehicular liberty often consists of no more than the right to be by yourself in a traffic jam, it's easy to imagine, and to envy vividly, our own motoring grandparents.

Edith Wharton was quite unconcerned about all mechanical aspects of the magical marvel; but she grasped clearly what Percy Lubbock called 'the opportunity of its power'. As he put it, she 'remained an example to all for the intelligence with which she worked the capacity of her slave. It played an honourable, never obtrusive or assertive part in innumerable excursions' – in England, France, Italy and the States. It also brought unexpected creative benefits. In her autobiography *A Backward Glance*, Wharton describes her early American motoring adventures, and how 'one would set out on a ten-mile run with more apprehension than would now attend a journey across Africa.' Gradually, she began to make longer and longer sorties into the remote blue hills of Massachusetts and New Hampshire, 'discovering derelict villages with Georgian churches and balustraded house-fronts, exploring slumbrous mountain valleys, and coming back, weary but laden with a new harvest of beauty.' Laden, as it turned out, with more than this: for it was the suddenly possible exploration of these 'villages still bedrowsed in a decaying rural existence', filled with 'sad slow-speaking people', that provoked her masterly novel *Ethan Frome*, as well as its warmer pendant *Summer*.

In this American phase Edith Wharton and her husband Teddy got through numerous motors: 'selling, buying and exchanging went on continually, though without appreciably better results'. The three journeys described in *A Motor-Flight through France* were all undertaken in the same secondhand 15hp Panhard bought by Teddy in London. Literary – and perhaps automobilistic – decorum prevents her giving us details of punctures, oil-changes and breakdowns; social decorum from giving us details of fellow passengers. The first flight, a two week run down from Boulogne to Clermont-Ferrand and back to Paris, took place in May 1906 with Edith's brother Harry Jones for company; the second, a big circle of the South-West, the Pyrenees and the Rhône Valley, occupied just over three weeks of March–April 1907, with Henry James as fellow passenger; for the third, a quick dash into Picardy over the Whitsun weekend in 1907, Edith and Teddy were unaccompanied. Their regular chauffeur was Charles Cook, a man of 'native Yankee saneness and intelligence', according to Henry James. Wharton wrote up the flights for the *Atlantic Monthly*, and collected them into the present volume, first published in October 1908.

There is a famous photograph, taken in Paris in 1907, of the Wharton Panhard and its occupants. The begoggled Cook is at the wheel, dutifully and sternly inspecting the road ahead; Teddy Wharton is at his side holding up two small dogs to the camera; while in the back sit Edith and an unsmiling, check-capped Henry James. They seem poised to launch themselves at what Wharton called the 'enchanting motor-grounds' of France, unencumbered, free as birds. Pedants, however, will note that there is little room in the Panhard for any luggage; and besides, it is hard to imagine either Edith Wharton or the 64-year-old James toting their own trunks. There was, in fact, much textually suppressed domestic support on these motor-flights: half a dozen servants went ahead by train or van and prepared for the subsequent arrival of the principals. Writing from the Grand Hotel in Pau while Teddy Wharton was laid up with bronchitis, James described this aspect of their travels in a typical parenthetical curlicue: 'My hosts are full of amenity, sympathy, appreciation, etc., (as well as of wondrous other servanted and avant-courier'd arts of travel).'

Another misapprehension would be to assume that James – elderly, distinguished, yet not rich – was the guest of the younger and much richer Whartons. In fact, he paid his own way, and the hotels de luxe which his hosts automatically patronized put him to financial strain. As he admitted in another letter from Pau, he was living 'an expensive fairy-tale', learning once again how it was always 'one's rich friends who cost one'. He realized with apprehension that by the end of the trip there would be six servants, plus chauffeur Cook, to tip. James evidently forbore to mention such embarrass-ments to the Whartons, although Edith would certainly have had a general awareness of his financially subservient state. Percy Lubbock tells a story of the two writers taking a drive in Edith Wharton's motor – a new one bought, she happens to mention, with the proceeds of her last novel. 'With the proceeds of *my* last novel,' James replies meditatively, 'I purchased a small go-cart, or hand-barrow, on which my guests' luggage is wheeled from the station to my house. With the proceeds of my next novel I shall have it painted.'

The early motorist had to be an adventurous stoic. The 1900 Michelin guide, alongside various remedies for mechan-ical ills, lists its special formula for 'driver's eye-lotion' (450 g infusion of coca leaves, 25 g cherry-laurel water, 15 g biborate

4

of soda). Wharton's very first motoring experience – a thrilling hundred-mile round trip from Rome to the Villa Caparola in 1903 – left her with two afflictions: acute motor-fever and acute laryngitis, the latter keeping her in bed for several days. On subsequent expeditions she was obliged, even in the hottest weather, to take the precaution of being 'swaddled in a stifling hood with a mica window, till some benefactor of the race invented the windscreen and made motoring an unmixed joy'. The Wharton windscreen appears to have arrived between the first and second motor-flights. For the 1906 trip they went unscreened and were pursued by rain ('It has been a cold, dark dreary spring in Europe, owing to Vesuvius they say'), and in the famous auto-shot of 1907 the Panhard still has no protection: James is hunched in a big fur coat, while Edith Wharton is much turbaned and scarfed, and may even be sporting her mica peephole. But we know that at some point before departure for the south Teddy Wharton personally made modifications to the car, closing in the body, installing interior electric light, and adding 'every known accessorie and comfort'.

It was Henry James who proposed himself as companion on the second and longest of these motor-flights. When he heard about the previous year's flight – and in particular about the visit to George Sand's house at Nohant – he reacted with parodic yet real jealousy. He had, he wrote to Edith, 'a strange telepathic intuition. A few days after you sloped off to France I said to myself suddenly: "They're on their way to Nohant, d—n them! They're going there – they *are* there!"' Such envy is understandable: during his younger days in Paris, James had met Flaubert, Gautier and Maupassant, all of whom had described to him the Second Empire's most famous literary pilgrimage – then made by train and diligence – to visit *la mère*

Sand. Now, writing from the Reform Club in November 1906, James begs Wharton to recount 'Your adventure and impressions of Nohant – as to which I burn and yearn for fond particulars. Perhaps if you have the proper Vehicle of Passion – as I make no doubt – you will be going there once more – in which case *do* take me!' This request accounts for the only narrative duplication in the book; though James's presence on the second visit helped gain them access to the interior of the house.

On 20 March 1907 the Whartons and James, with Cook at the wheel, set off from Paris in the Vehicle of Passion. This was James's generic sobriquet for the Wharton motor; individual engines had their particular nicknames, such as 'the Chariot of Fire' and 'Hortense' (after the erotic novelist Hortense Allart). The journey must have had an extra edge of shading for James, because exactly a quarter of a century earlier, in 1882, he had himself made *A Little Tour in France*, which he had also published in periodical then hard-bound form. Many of the places he had visited then he was to revisit with the Whartons, especially on the southern section: Angoûleme, Bordeaux, Toulouse, Carcassonne, Nîmes, Avignon, Bourg-en-Bresse and Dijon. Leon Edel characterizes his Tour as 'neat, well-placed, inexpensive'; now he was involved in the whirl and luxury of the Whartons. His had been a typically nineteenth-century journey: by train and horse to squalid inn. Now there was the Vehicle of Passion speeding you to a hotel which, if it failed to reach Edith's high expectations, was rejected. Sometimes a whole town was unfit for Whartonian overnighting. Sometimes a whole region: in central France, she notes, 'one is often doomed to pine' for 'digestible food and clean beds'. Motoring also permitted the fastidious to indulge a certain topographical snobbery. There was no need to approach a town through the 'mean purlieus' of the railway station, the 'area of ugliness and desolation created by the railway itself'; now your first impression of a place could once again – as for your 'posting grandparents' – be 'romantic or stately'. This cocooning effect extends, however, beyond the mere matter of marshalling yards: speed, the motor, chosen *compagnons de voyage* and avant-courier'd servants all minimize the kind of chance human contact thrown up by earlier, slower, solitary travelling. Wharton's book chronicles peasant faces glimpsed in doorways and the flushed servant at the auberge, but it's significant that the two largest human presences in her text are both long dead: George Sand and Madame de Sévigné.

James's *Little Tour* is inclined to make us nostalgic for that era of leisurely, meticulous yet also somewhat lazy travel, our guide a highly sophisticated man taking his sensibility, like some great dog, for a walk. *A Motor-Flight* is the work of a genuine modern tourist. Someone with just as much art and sensibility as James, but closer to us; someone facing – and choosing to face – a hastier flurry of sense impressions, a quicker mental satiety; someone also whose activities, unlike those of the solitary ruin-bibber, are going to change the land under inspection. 'The demands of motoring are introducing modern plumbing and Maple furniture into the uttermost parts of France,' Wharton acknowledges. Those romantic old inns, where it is 'charming to breakfast, if precarious to sleep', are already doomed.

Although Wharton presents herself as 'the trivial motorist, the mere snarer of haphazard impressions', we should not be misled by this self-presentation as an aesthetic amateur. The French cathedrals were for her vivid embodiments of architectural principles long understood and digested, rather than (as for the true trivial motorist) a jumbled assemblage of elements for which the guidebook must supply the crossword solution. When she discusses the 'hale durability' of the Romanesque, laments – contentiously – that France 'has never wholly understood the use of brick', drops an aside about what English Gothic lost by committing itself to the square east end; when she disentangles the Crusader church at Neuvy-Saint-Sépulcre, luxuriates in the façade of Rheims cathedral, wittily castigates the 'hairless pink monster' at Albi; when she decries the work of Viollet-le-Duc without being so doctrinaire as to ignore his occasional coups; when she praises the benign neglect of buildings, which allows them to show their 'scars and hues of age' rather than appearing as spruce old ladies; when she invokes the aesthetic centrality of the Italian hill-town whose architecture embellishes and completes the contours of the landscape – on such occasions we attend to an authority, not to a mere motorist.

At the same time – and this is part of what makes her close to us – she is not content to treat the successive edifices before her like some version of wine-tasting, an occasion for fine minds with fine purses to display their fine discriminations. What does it, can it, should it mean for a person of a later, swifter civilization to examine these remnants of an earlier, slower yet surer civilization? Can we view them imaginatively, or only solipsistically? What sort of pleasure, what rousing to reverence can we legitimately expect? She addresses such questions at the start of the book, at Amiens, and returns to them near its close, at Rheims. She was skilled at focusing them because – like James – she was aware of coming from 'a land which has undertaken to get on without a past', whose citizen-tourists at large in Europe were inclined to treat the architectural expression of vast historical forces as a mere aesthetic diversion. This approach is even commoner now-adays, and we should all be rebuked and enlightened by Wharton's example.

She is, indeed, that rare and oxymoronic thing, the wise tourist; one eager to give an account of 'what he sees, and *feels beneath the thing seen*' (the italics, as well as the masculine pronoun, are hers). She has great powers of mental compari-son: leaving Beauvais, she finds that she has not really quitted it because she is still – and her phrase is scentedly Jamesian – 'imprisoned in that tremendous memory'. She treasures build-ings that carry the imagination back in a direct flight, to a time when 'piety still walked with art'. Tourism for her is thus not passive but constructive, re-creative. There is a completeness as well as a wisdom to her: she moves easily between landscape, architecture and humanity, treating them as over-lapping rather than self-contained areas of study; she can do that hardest of art-critical jobs, which is to make tapestries sound interesting; and just when you think she might be coasting she will be sparklingly descriptive. The carved mer-maids on the choir-stalls of Saint Savin leap out at us as 'creatures of bale and beauty, who seem to have brought from across the Alps their pagan eyes and sidelong Lombard smile'; the Pyrenees, when viewed from the taming distance of the terrace at Pau, are 'subjected to a kind of indignity of inspection, like caged carnivora in a zoo'.

But it would be a mistake to represent her either as a natural praiser – she is robustly dismissive of Toulouse and the vulgarity of Lourdes, of false decoration and meretricious bedizening – or as a mere building-broker. Her landscapes are vivid, and peopled with a peasantry she attends to carefully, if lyrically. When she writes of Pyrenean hill-country men 'so disciplined by industry, yet so romantically free', or of the

French provincial face provoking 'the same kind of interest as a work of art', we should, I think, be overhasty in thinking her just another rich urban foreigner charmed by local colour. What she finds in these glimpsed physiognomies is what she also seeks and celebrates in old buildings: something that carries the imagination back in a direct flight. Perhaps she is aware (without stating it) that the motorist who arrives in the uttermost parts of France with an expectation of modern plumbing and Maple furniture is also finally a menace to the 'independence and simplicity of living', the 'thriftily compact traditional life' which has over centuries formed and defined the landscape's inhabitants. What she celebrates about France on the human side is its civic order and elegance, the amenity of manners, the vivacity, good temper and intelligent enjoyment of life. These terms are always comparative, of course. Nowadays the motorist will find that the approaches to French towns are no more 'romantic or stately' by road than they are by rail; and just as there is a commercial clutter of Monsieur Bricolage and his confrères disfiguring the out-skirts, so there is more of an overlay, as elsewhere, to the perceptible character of the people. We can no longer see back as clearly.

Wharton and James agreed about much, but not everything, of what they saw together. Each had an aesthetic in which Italy was the touchstone; they liked their old buildings old, and were suspicious of restoration. She is more wholehearted in admiring the Graeco-Roman remains of Provence (he judges the Pont du Gard finally 'a little stupid', and finds a magnificent phrase with which to diminish Roman architec-ture: 'The Roman rigidity was apt to overshoot the mark, and I suppose a race which could do nothing small is as defective as a race that can do nothing great'). He loathes Avignon; she

finds it engagingly Italianate. But their most instructive dis-
agreement comes at Bourg-en-Bresse, whose principal attraction is the church at Brou.

James's account begins with a sentimental evocation of
Matthew Arnold's then-celebrated poem about Brou. He
twits and pardons Arnold for his geographical inexactitude,
sketches the flamboyant piety that lay behind the construction
of the church, dabbles with his guide-book, describes the
famous tombs, gives them little butter-dabs of approval –
admirable, admirable, charming, exquisite, splendid, ingeni-
ous, elaborate, precious – before concluding that, though fine,
the monuments are not quite so fine as their rivals in Verona.
He makes a slightly arch mother-in-law joke, marvels that the
whole edifice wasn't destroyed in the Revolution, and segues
effortlessly into a rhapsodic description – more fun for us, and,
one senses, for him too – of the simple yet epicurean lunch of
boiled eggs, bread and local butter that he subsequently
consumed in Bourg.

Wharton's account makes no reference to James's text of
1882, any more than it does to his living presence beside her
in the Panhard twenty-five years later. It must have been
intimidating to address an unchanged subject already discussed
by an accompanying Master. No doubt she had read *A Little
Tour*; though when last, we do not know. How could there
not be, at some level, an element of competitiveness in her
description? She too begins with Arnold's poem, which she
treats with brisk jocundity, wondering if he could ever have
seen the church at Brou, so inaccurately does he locate it. As
for the edifice itself: for a start, it disobeys Wharton's precept
that old buildings should look old – this one is 'scrubbed,
scraped and soaped as if its renovation were a feat daily
performed by the "seven maids with seven mops" on whose

purifying powers the walrus so ingeniously speculated'. Externally, it is 'a celluloid toy'. Internally, it reminds her of the Albert Memorial, all pious expense and little taste. It is 'pastrycook's art'. Alongside this rough journalistic abuse resides her precise architectural sense. Where James murmurs suavely that Margaret of Austria's shrine is 'the last extravagance of a Gothic which had gone so far that nothing was left it but to return upon itself', Wharton makes the same point in a more vernacular style ('the last boiling-over of the heterogeneous Gothic pot'), emphasizes her extra knowledge ('One sees the same result in almost all the monuments of the period, especially where the Spanish-Netherlands influence has added a last touch of profusion'), and seals it with a memorable metaphor: 'Expiring Gothic changed its outline as often as the dying dolphin is supposed to change his colours – every ornament suggests a convulsion in stone.' And whereas James moves lightly on to lunch, Wharton moves seriously on to a comparison with the mourning sculptures on the tomb of Jean-sans-Peur in Dijon, which she values highly (and which James had found of 'limited interest'). A leery mind might hazard that despite her true reverence for James, she is out to pull architectural rank; while also ensuring that her freshness of tone impresses him with her modernity.

James occasionally made fond mock of Edith Wharton's travel-fever, portraying her as a bossy bird of prey swooping down on the more sedentary and bearing them off 'on india-rubber wings'. But they were clearly excellent and devoted companions en voyage. James reported that on the motor-flight he had 'almost the time of my life', and looking back he gave out gratified exhalations. 'Ah, the lovely rivers and the inveterately glorious grub.' 'Ah, the good food and good manners and good looks everywhere!' For her part, Edith

Wharton declared that 'Never was there a more admirable travelling companion, more ready to enjoy and unready to find fault – never bored, never disappointed, and never (*need* I say?) missing any of the little fine touches of sensation that enrich the moments of the really good traveller.' No sooner had they got back to Paris than she whisked him away for another brief flight. And it was James again in April 1908 who responds enthusiastically to the idea of meeting in Amiens with the suggestion of 'a little *tournée*, under motor-goggles, in Normandy'. He has a specific and powerful destination in mind: '& oh, will you take me to Croisset, by Rouen, as a pendant to Nohant?' It would indeed have been a fitting pendant – first Sand's house, then the vestiges of Flaubert's – but the plan fell victim to the complications of Wharton's emotional life.

One final motor trip should, however, be mentioned. Shortly after the publication of *A Motor-Flight through France* the two novelists were driving from Rye to Windsor when James suggested making a detour to Box Hill to visit the aged George Meredith. Wharton was at first unwilling, as she judged herself unlikely to shine in such impromptu circumstances; then she agreed to the route-change but insisted upon staying in the car at Box Hill. Determinedly, James overcame her objections and took her with him into the house. Meredith, terminally ill, deeply deaf, and 'statuesquely enthroned in a Bath chair', had great difficulty cracking the identity of this unknown woman who had turned up unexpectedly with Henry James. It was, she later recalled, 'a laborious business, and agonizing to me, as the room rang again and again with my unintelligible name'. Eventually, Meredith twigged; whereupon he picked up the book lying open at his elbow, and held it out with a smile. 'I read the title, and the blood rushed over me like fire. It was my own *Motor-Flight through France*, then lately published; and he had not known I was to be brought to see him, and he had actually been reading my book when I came in!'

Julian Barnes

PART ONE

One
BOULOGNE TO AMIENS

T HE MOTOR-CAR has restored the romance of travel.

Freeing us from all the compulsions and contacts of the railway, the bondage to fixed hours and the beaten track, the approach to each town through the area of ugliness and desolation created by the railway itself, it has given us back the wonder, the adventure and the novelty which enlivened the way of our posting grandparents. Above all these recovered pleasures must be ranked the delight of taking a town unawares, stealing on it by back ways and unchronicled paths, and surprising in it some intimate aspect of past time, some silhouette hidden for half a century or more by the ugly mask of railway embankments and the iron bulk of a huge station. Then the villages that we missed and yearned for from the windows of the train – the unseen villages have been given back to us! – and nowhere could the importance of the recovery have been more delightfully exemplified than on a May afternoon in the Pas-de-Calais, as we climbed the long ascent beyond Boulogne on the road to Arras.

It is a delightful country, broken into wide waves of hill and valley, with hedge-rows high and leafy enough to bear comparison with the Kentish hedges among which our motor had left us a day or two before; and the villages, the frequent, smiling, happily placed villages, will also meet successfully the more serious challenge of their English rivals – meet it on other grounds and in other ways, with paved market-places

ARRAS: HÔTEL DE VILLE

and clipped *charmilles* instead of gorse-fringed commons, with
soaring belfries instead of square church towers, with less of
verdure, but more, perhaps, of outline – certainly of line.

The country itself – so green, so full and close in texture,
so pleasantly diversified by clumps of woodland in the hollows,
and by streams threading the great fields with light – all this,
too, has the English, or perhaps the Flemish quality – for the
border is close by – with the added beauty of reach and
amplitude, the deliberate gradual flow of level spaces into
distant slopes, till the land breaks in a long blue crest against
the seaward horizon.

There was much beauty of detail, also, in the smaller towns
through which we passed: some of them high-perched on
ridges that raked the open country, with old houses stumbling
down at picturesque angles from the central market-place;
others tucked in the hollows, among orchards and barns, with
the pleasant country industries reaching almost to the doors of
their churches. In the little villages a deep delicious thatch
overhangs the plastered walls of cottages espaliered with pear-
trees, and ducks splash in ponds fringed with hawthorn and
laburnum; and in the towns there is almost always some note
of character, of distinction – the gateway of a seventeenth-
century *hôtel*, the triple arch of a church-front, the spring of
an old mossy apse, the stucco and black cross-beams of an
ancient guild-house – and always the straight lime-walk,
square-clipped or trained *en berceau*, with its sharp green angles
and sharp black shade acquiring a value positively architectural
against the high lights of the paved or gravelled *place*. Everything about this rich juicy land bathed in blond light is
characteristically Flemish, even to the slow-moving eyes of
the peasants, the bursting red cheeks of the children, the
drowsy grouping of the cattle in flat pastures; and at Hesdin

we felt the architectural nearness of the Low Countries in the presence of a fine town hall of the late Renaissance, with the peculiar 'movement' of volutes and sculptured ornament — lime-stone against warm brick — that one associates with the civic architecture of Belgium: a fuller, less sensitive line than the French architect permits himself, with more massiveness and exuberance of detail.

This part of France, with its wide expanse of agricultural landscape, disciplined and cultivated to the last point of finish, shows how nature may be utilized to the utmost clod without losing its freshness and naturalness. In some regions of this supremely 'administered' country, where space is more restricted, or the fortunate accidents of water and varying levels are lacking, the minute excessive culture, the endless ranges of *potager* wall, and the long lines of fruit-trees bordering straight interminable roads, may produce in the American traveller a reaction toward the unkempt, a momentary feeling that ragged road-sides and weedy fields have their artistic value. But here in northern France, where agriculture has mated with poetry instead of banishing it, one understands the higher beauty of land developed, humanized, brought into relation to life and history, as compared with the raw material with which the greater part of our own hemisphere is still clothed. In France everything speaks of long familiar intercourse between the earth and its inhabitants; every field has a name, a history, a distinct place of its own in the village polity; every blade of grass is there by an old feudal right which has long since dispossessed the worthless aboriginal weed.

As we neared Arras the road lost its pleasant windings and ran straight across a great plateau, with an occasional long dip and ascent that never deflected it from its purpose, and the villages became rarer, as they always do on the high wind-

swept plains of France. Arras, however, was full of compensations for the dullness of the approach: a charming old grey
town, with a great air of faded seventeenth-century opulence,
in which one would have liked to linger, picking out details
of gateway and courtyard, of sculptured masks and wrought-
iron balconies – if only a brief peep into the hotel had not so
promptly quenched the impulse to spend a night there.

To Amiens therefore we passed on, passing again, toward
sunset, into a more broken country, with lights just beginning
to gleam through the windows of the charming duck-pond
villages, and tall black crucifixes rising ghostly at the crossroads;
and night was obliterating the mighty silhouette of the
cathedral as we came upon it at length by a long descent.

It is always a loss to arrive in a strange town after dark, and
miss those preliminary stages of acquaintance that are so much
more likely to be interesting in towns than in people; but the
deprivation is partly atoned for by the sense of adventure with
which, next morning, one casts one's self upon the unknown.
There is no conjectural first impression to be modified,
perhaps got rid of: one's mind presents a blank page for the
town to write its name on.

At Amiens the autograph consists of one big word: the
cathedral. Other, fainter writing may come out when one has
leisure to seek for it; but the predominance of those mighty
characters leaves, at first, no time to read between the lines.
And here it may be noted that, out of Italy, it takes a town of
exceptional strength of character to hold its own against a
cathedral. In England, the chapter house and the varied
groupings of semi-ecclesiastical buildings constituting the
close, which seem to form a connecting link between town
and cathedral, do no more, in reality, than enlarge the skirts
of the monument about which they are clustered; and even

AMIENS: WEST FRONT OF THE CATHEDRAL

at Winchester, which has its college and hospital to oppose to the predominance of the central pile, there is, after all, very little dispersal of interest: so prodigious, so unparalleled, as mere feats of human will power, are these vast achievements of the Middle Ages. In northern France, where the great cathedrals were of lay foundation, and consequently sprang up alone, without the subordinate colony of monastic buildings of which the close is a survival – and where, as far as monuments of any importance are concerned, the architectural gap sometimes extends from Louis the Saint to Louis the Fourteenth – the ascendancy of the diocesan church is necessarily even more marked. Rouen alone, perhaps, opposes an effectual defence to this concentration of interest, will not for a moment let itself be elbowed out of the way by the great buttresses of its cathedral; and at Bourges – but Bourges and Rouen come later in this itinerary, and meanwhile here we are, standing, in a sharp shower, under a *notaire*'s doorway, and looking across the little square at the west front of Amiens.

Well! No wonder such a monument has silenced all competitors. It would take a mighty counterblast to make itself heard against 'the surge and thunder' of that cloud of witnesses choiring forth the glories of the Church Triumphant. Is the stage too crowded? Is there a certain sameness in the overarching tiers of the stone hierarchy, each figure set in precise alignment with its neighbours, each drapery drawn within the same perpendicular bounds? Yes, perhaps – if one remembers Rheims and Bourges; but if, setting aside such kindred associations, one surrenders one's self uncritically to the total impression produced, if one lets the fortunate accidents of time and weather count for their full value in that total – for Amiens remains mercifully unscrubbed, and its armies of saints have taken on the richest *patina* that northern stone can acquire – if one views the thing, in short, partly as a symbol and partly as a 'work of nature' (which all ancient monuments by grace of time become), then the front of Amiens is surely one of the most splendid spectacles that Gothic art can show.

On the symbolic side especially it would be tempting to linger; so strongly does the contemplation of the great cathedrals fortify the conviction that their chief value, to this later age, is not so much æsthetic as moral. The world will doubtless always divide itself into two orders of mind: that which sees in past expressions of faith, political, religious or intellectual, only the bonds cast off by the spirit of man in its long invincible struggle for 'more light'; and that which, while moved by the spectacle of the struggle, cherishes also every sign of those past limitations that were, after all, each in its turn, symbols of the same effort toward a clearer vision. To the former kind of mind the great Gothic cathedral will be chiefly interesting as a work of art and a page of history; and it is perhaps proof of the advantage of cultivating the other – the more complex – point of view, in which enfranchisement of thought exists in harmony with atavism of feeling, that it permits one to appreciate these archæological values to the full, yet subordinates them to the more impressive facts of which they are the immense and moving expression. To such minds, the rousing of the sense of reverence is the supreme gift of these mighty records of mediæval life: reverence for the persistent, slow-moving, far-reaching forces that brought them forth. A great Gothic cathedral sums up so much of history, it has cost so much in faith and toil, in blood and folly and saintly abnegation, it has sheltered such a long succession of lives, given collective voice to so many inarticulate and

AMIENS: AMBULATORY OF THE CATHEDRAL

contradictory cravings, seen so much that was sublime and terrible, or foolish, pitiful and grotesque, that it is like some mysteriously preserved ancestor of the human race, some Wandering Jew grown sedentary and throned in stony contemplation, before whom the fleeting generations come and go.

Yes – reverence is the most precious emotion that such a building inspires: reverence for the accumulated experiences of the past, readiness to puzzle out their meaning, unwillingness to disturb rashly results so powerfully willed, so laboriously arrived at – the desire, in short, to keep intact as many links as possible between yesterday and tomorrow, to lose, in the ardour of new experiment, the least that may be of the long rich heritage of human experience. This, at any rate, might seem to be the cathedral's word to the traveller from a land which has undertaken to get on without the past, or to regard it only as a 'feature' of æsthetic interest, a sight to which one travels rather than a light by which one lives.

The west front of Amiens says this word with a quite peculiar emphasis, its grand unity of structure and composition witnessing as much to constancy of purpose as to persistence of effort. So steadily, so clearly, was this great thing willed and foreseen, that it holds the mind too deeply subject to its general conception to be immediately free for the delighted investigation of detail. But within the building detail reasserts itself: detail within detail, worked out and multiplied with a prodigality of enrichment for which a counterpart must be sought beyond the Alps. The interiors of the great French cathedrals are as a rule somewhat gaunt and unfurnished, baring their structural nakedness sublimely but rather monotonously to eyes accustomed to the Italian churches 'all glorious within'. Here at Amiens, however, the inner decking of the

shrine has been piously continued from generation to generation, and a quite extraordinary wealth of adornment bestowed
on the choir and its ambulatory. The great sculptured and
painted frieze encircling the outer side of the choir is especially
surprising in a French church, so seldom were the stone
histories lavished on the exterior continued within the building; and it is a further surprise to find the same tales in bas-
relief animating and enriching the west walls of the transepts.
They are full of crowded expressive incidents, these stories of
local saints and Scriptural personages; with a Burgundian
richness and elaborateness of costume, and a quite charming,
childish insistence on irrelevant episode and detail − the
reiterated 'And so', 'And then' of the fairy-tale calling off
one's attention into innumerable little by-paths, down which
the fancy of fifteenth-century worshippers must have strayed,
with oh! what blessedness of relief, from the unintelligible
rites before the altar.

Of composition there is none: it is necessarily sacrificed to
the desire to stop and tell everything; to show, for instance, in
an interesting parenthesis, exactly what Herod's white woolly
dog was about while Salome was dancing away the Baptist's
head. And thus one is brought back to the perpetually
recurring fact that all northern art is anecdotic, and has always
been so; and that, for instance, all the elaborate theories of
dramatic construction worked out to explain why Shakespeare
crowded his stage with subordinate figures and unnecessary
incidents, and would certainly, in relating the story of Saint
John, have included Herod's 'Tray and Sweetheart' among
the dramatis personæ − that such theories are but an unprofitable evasion of the ancient ethnological fact *that the Goth has
always told his story in that way.*

BEAUVAIS: WEST FRONT OF THE CATHEDRAL

Two
BEAUVAIS AND ROUEN

THE SAME WONDERFUL white road, flinging itself in great coils and arrow-flights across the same spacious landscape, swept us on the next day to Beauvais. If there seemed to be fewer memorable incidents by the way – if the villages had less individual character, over and above their general charm of northern thrift and cosiness – it was perhaps because the first impression had lost its edge; but we caught fine distant reaches of field and orchard and wooded hillside, giving a general sense that it would be a good land to live in – till all these minor sensations were swallowed up and lost in the overwhelming impression of Beauvais.

The town itself – almost purposely, as we felt afterward – failed to put itself forward, to arrest us by any of the minor arts which Arras, for instance, had so seductively exerted. It maintained an attitude of calm aloofness, of affected ignorance of the traveller's object in visiting it – suffering its little shuttered non-committal streets to lead us up, tortuously, to the drowsiest little provincial *place*, with the usual lime-arcades, and the usual low houses across the way; where suddenly there soared before us the great mad broken dream of Beauvais choir – the cathedral without a nave – the Kubla Khan of architecture . . .

It seems in truth like some climax of mystic vision, miraculously caught in visible form, and arrested, broken off, by the intrusion of the Person from Porlock – in this case, no doubt, the panic-stricken mason, crying out to the entranced creator: 'We simply can't keep it up!' And because it literally couldn't be kept up – as one or two alarming collapses soon attested – it had to check there its great wave of stone, hold itself for ever back from breaking into the long ridge of the nave and flying crests of buttress, spire and finial. It is easy for the critic to point out its structural defects, and to cite them in illustration of the fact that your true artist never seeks to wrest from their proper uses the materials in which he works – does not, for instance, try to render metaphysical abstractions in stone and glass and lead; yet Beauvais has at least none of the ungainliness of failure: it is like a great hymn interrupted, not one in which the voices have flagged; and to the desultory mind such attempts seem to deserve a place among the fragmentary glories of great art. It is, at any rate, an example of what the Gothic spirit, pushed to its logical conclusion, strove for: the utterance of the unutterable; and he who condemns Beauvais has tacitly condemned the whole theory of art from which it issued. But shall we not have gained greatly in our enjoyment of beauty, as well as in serenity of spirit, if, instead of saying 'this is good art', or 'this is bad art', we say 'this is classic' and 'that is Gothic' – this transcendental, that rational – using neither term as an epithet of opprobrium or restriction, but content, when we have performed the act of discrimination, to note what forms of expression each tendency has worked out for itself?

Beyond Beauvais the landscape became more deeply Norman – more thatched and green and orchard-smothered – though, as far as the noting of detail went, we did not really get *beyond Beauvais* at all, but travelled on imprisoned in that tremendous memory till abruptly, from the crest of a hill, we looked down a long green valley to Rouen shining on its river

– belfries, spires and great arched bridges drenched with a golden sunset that seemed to shoot skyward from the long illuminated reaches of the Seine. I recall only two such magic descents on famous towns: that on Orvieto, from the last hill of the Viterbo road, and the other – pitched in a minor key, but full of a small ancient majesty – the view of Wells in its calm valley, as the Bath road gains the summit of the Mendip hills.

The poetry of the descent to Rouen is, unhappily, dispelled by the long approach through sordid interminable outskirts. Orvieto and Wells, being less prosperous, do not subject the traveller to this descent into prose, which leaves one reflecting mournfully on the incompatibility, under our present social system, between prosperity and beauty. As for Rouen itself, as one passes down its crowded tram-lined quays, between the noisy unloading of ships and the clatter of innumerable cafés, one feels that the old Gothic town one used to know cannot really exist any more, must have been elbowed out of place by these spreading commercial activities; but it turns out to be there, after all, holding almost intact, behind the dull mask of modern streets, the surprise of its rich mediævalism.

Here indeed the traveller finds himself in no mere 'cathedral town'; with one street leading to Saint Ouen, another to Saint Maclou, a third to the beautiful Palais de Justice, the cathedral itself has put forth the appeal of all its accumulated treasures to make one take, first of all, the turn to its doors. There are few completer impressions in Europe than that to be received as one enters the Lady Chapel of Rouen, where an almost Italian profusion of colour and ornament have been suffered to accumulate slowly about its central ornament – the typically northern monument of the two Cardinals of Amboise. There could hardly be a better

ROUEN: RUE DE L'HORLOGE

example of the æsthetic wisdom of 'living and letting live' than is manifested by the happy way in which supposedly incompatible artistic ideals have contrived to make *bon ménage* in this delicious corner. It is a miracle that they have been allowed to pursue their happy experiment till now, for there must have been moments when, to the purist of the Renaissance, the Gothic tomb of the Cardinals seemed unworthy to keep company with the Sénéchal de Brézé's monument, in which the delicate note of classicalism reveals a France so profoundly modified by Italy; just as, later, the great Berniniesque altar-piece, with its twisted columns and exuberance of golden rays, must have narrowly escaped the axe of the Gothic reactionary. But there they all are, blending their supposed discords in a more complex harmony, filling the privileged little edifice with an overlapping richness of hue and line through which the eye perpetually passes back to the central splendour of the Cardinals' tomb.

A magnificent monument it is, opposing to the sober beauty of Germain Pilon's composition its insolence of varied detail – the 'this, and this, and this' of the loquacious mediæval craftsman – all bound together by the new constructive sense which has already learned how to bring the topmost bud of the marble finials into definite relation with the little hooded mourners bowed in such diversity of grief in their niches below the tomb. A magnificent monument – and to my mind the finest thing about it is the Cardinal Uncle's nose. The whole man is fine in his sober dignity, humbly conscious of the altar toward which he faces, arrogantly aware of the purple on his shoulders; and the nose is the epitome of the man. We live in the day of little noses: that once stately feature, intrinsically feudal and aristocratic in character – the *maschio naso* extolled of Dante – has shrunk to democratic insignificance, like many another fine expression of individualism. And so one must look to the old painters and sculptors to see what a nose was meant to be – the prow of the face; the evidence of its owner's standing, of his relation to the world, and his inheritance from the past. Even in the profile of the Cardinal Nephew, kneeling a little way behind his uncle, the gallant feature is seen to have suffered a slight diminution: its spring, still bold, is less commanding; it seems, as it were, to have thrust itself against a less yielding element. And so the deterioration has gone on from generation to generation, till the nose has worn itself blunt against the increasing resistances of a democratic atmosphere, and stunted, atrophied and amorphous, serves only, now, to let us know when we have the influenza.

With the revisiting of the Cardinal's nose the first object of our visit to Rouen had been accomplished; the second led us, past objects of far greater importance, to the well-arranged but dull gallery where Gerhard David's *Virgin of the Grapes* is to be seen. Every wanderer through the world has these pious pilgrimages to perform, generally to shrines of no great note – how often, for instance, is one irresistibly drawn back to the Transfiguration or to the Venus of Milo? – but to lesser works, first seen, perhaps, at a fortunate moment, or having some special quality of suggestion and evocation that the perfect equilibrium of the masterpieces causes them to lack. So I know of some who go first to *The Death of Procris* in the National Gallery; to the little *Apollo and Marsyas* of the Salon Carré; to a fantastic allegorical picture, subject and artist unknown, in an obscure corner of the Uffizi; and who would travel more miles to see again, in the little gallery of Rimini, an Entombment of the school of Mantegna, than to sit beneath the vault of the Sistine.

ROUEN: THE FAÇADE OF THE CATHEDRAL OF SAINT-MACLOU

All of which may seem to imply an unintentional disparagement of Gerhard David's picture, which is, after all, a masterpiece of its school; but the school is a subordinate one, and, save to the student of Flemish art, his is not a loud-sounding name: one does not say, for instance, with any hope of general recognition – 'Ah, yes; that reminds me of such and such a bit in *The Virgin of the Grapes*.'

All the more, therefore, may one enjoy his picture, in the empty room of the Rouen gallery, with that gentle sense of superiority and possessorship to which the discerner of obscure merit is surely entitled. How much of its charm this particular painting owes to its not having become the picnic-ground of the art-excursionist, how much to its own intrinsic beauty, its grave serenities of hue and gesture – how much, above all, to the heavenly translucence of that bunch of grapes plucked from the vines of Paradise – it is part of its very charm to leave unsettled, to keep among the mysteries whereby it draws one back. Only one trembles lest it should cease to shine in its own twilight heaven when it has become a star in Baedeker . . .

Three
FROM ROUEN TO
FONTAINEBLEAU

T HE SEINE, TWO days later, by the sweetest curves, drew
us on from Rouen to Les Andelys, past such bright
gardens terraced above its banks, such moist poplar-fringed
islands, such low green promontories deflecting its silver flow,
that we continually checked the flight of the motor, pausing
here, and here, and here again, to note how France understands and enjoys and lives with her rivers.

With her great past, it seems, she has partly ceased to live;
for, ask as we would, we could not, that morning, learn the
way to King Richard's Château Gaillard on the cliff above Les
Andelys. Every turn from the route de Paris seemed to lead
straight into the unknown; *'mais c'est tout droit pour Paris'* was
the invariable answer when we asked our way. Yet a few
miles off were two of the quaintest towns of France – the
Little and Great Andely – surmounted by a fortress marking
an epoch in military architecture, and associated with the
fortunes of one of the most romantic figures in history; and
we knew that if we clung to the windings of the Seine they
must lead us, within a few miles, to the place we sought. And
so, having with difficulty disentangled ourselves from the
route de Paris, we pushed on, by quiet by-roads and unknown
villages, by *manoirs* of grey stone peeping through high thickets
of lilac and laburnum, and along shady river-reaches where
fishermen dozed in their punts, and cattle in the meadow-
grass beneath the willows – till the soft slopes broke abruptly

into tall cliffs shaggy with gorse, and the easy flow of the river was forced into a sharp twist at their base. There is something fantastic in this sudden change of landscape near Les Andelys from the familiar French river-scenery to what might be one of Piero della Francesca's backgrounds of strangely fretted rock and scant black vegetation; while the Seine, roused from its progress through yielding meadows, takes a majestic bend toward the Little Andely in the bay of the cliffs, and then sweeps out below the height on which Cœur-de-Lion planted his subtly calculated bastions.

Ah – poor fluttering rag of a ruin, so thin, so time-worn, so riddled with storm and shell, that it droops on its rock like a torn banner with forgotten victories in its folds! How much more eloquently these tottering stones tell their story, how much deeper into the past they take us, than the dapper weather-tight castles – Pierrefonds, Langeais, and the rest – on which the arch-restorer has worked his will, reducing them to mere museum specimens, archæological toys, from which all the growths of time have been ruthlessly stripped! The eloquence of the Château Gaillard lies indeed just there – in its telling us so discursively, so plaintively, the *whole* story of the centuries – how long it has stood, how much it has seen, how far the world has travelled since then, and to what a hoarse, cracked whisper the voice of feudalism and chivalry has dwindled . . .

The town that once cowered under the protection of those fallen ramparts still groups its stout old houses about a church so grey and venerable, yet so sturdily planted on its ancient piers, that one might fancy its compassionately bidding the poor ghost of a fortress come down and take shelter beneath its vaultings. Commune and castle, they have changed places with the shifting fortunes of the centuries, the weak growth

ROUEN: MONUMENT OF THE CARDINALS OF AMBOISE
IN THE CATHEDRAL

of the town outstripping the arrogant brief bloom of the fortress – Richard's 'fair daughter of one year' – which had called it arbitrarily into being. The fortress itself is now no more than one of the stage-properties of the Muse of History; but the town, poor little accidental offshoot of a military exigency, has built up a life for itself, become an abiding centre of human activities – though, by an accident in which the traveller cannot but rejoice, it still keeps, in spite of its sound masonry and air of ancient health, that almost unmodernized aspect which makes some little French burghs recall the figure of a lively centenarian, all his faculties still active, but wearing the dress of a former day.

Regaining the route de Paris, we passed once more into the normal Seine landscape, with smiling towns close-set on its shores, with lilac and wistaria pouring over high walls, with bright little cafés on sunny village squares, with flotillas of pleasure-boats moored under willow-shaded banks.

Never more vividly than in this Seine country does one feel the amenity of French manners, the long process of social adaptation which has produced so profound and general an intelligence of life. Everyone we passed on our way, from the canal-boatman to the white-capped baker's lad, from the *marchande des quatre saisons* to the white dog curled philosophically under her cart, from the pastry-cook putting a fresh plate of *brioches* in his appetizing window to the curé's *bonne* who had just come out to drain the lettuce on the curé's doorstep – all these persons (under which designation I specifically include the dog) took their ease or pursued their business with that cheerful activity which proceeds from an intelligent acceptance of given conditions. They each had their established niche in life, the frankly avowed interests and preoccupations of their order, their pride in the smartness of the canal-boat, the seductions of the show-window, the glaze of the *brioches*, the crispness of the lettuce. And this admirable *fitting into the pattern*, which seems almost as if it were a moral outcome of the universal French sense of form, has led the race to the happy, the momentous discovery that good manners are a short cut to one's goal, that they lubricate the wheels of life instead of obstructing them. This discovery – the result, as it strikes one, of the application of the finest of mental instruments to the muddled process of living – seems to have illuminated not only the social relation but its outward, concrete expression, producing a finish in the material setting of life, a kind of conformity in inanimate things – forming, in short, the background of the spectacle through which we pass, the canvas on which it is painted, and expressing itself no less in the trimness of each individual garden than in that insistence on civic dignity and comeliness so miraculously maintained, through every torment of political passion, every change of social conviction, by a people resolutely addressed to the intelligent enjoyment of living.

By Vernon, with its trim lime-walks *en berceau*, by Mantes with its bright gardens, and the graceful over-restored church which dominates its square, we passed on to Versailles, forsaking the course of the Seine that we might have a glimpse of the country about Fontainebleau.

At the top of the route du Buc, which climbs by sharp windings from the Place du Château at Versailles, one comes upon the arches of the aqueduct of Buc – one of the monuments of that splendid folly which created the 'Golden House' of Louis XIV, and drew its miraculous groves and gardens from the waterless plain of Versailles. The aqueduct, forming part of the extravagant scheme of irrigation of which the Machine de Marly and the great canal of Maintenon commemorate successive disastrous phases, frames, in its useless lofty openings, such charming glimpses of the country to the south-west of Versailles, that it takes its place among those abortive architectural experiments which seem, after all, to have been completely justified by time.

The landscape upon which the arches look is a high-lying region of wood and vale, with châteaux at the end of long green vistas, and old flowery villages tucked into folds of the hills. At the first turn of the road above Versailles the well-kept suburbanism of the Parisian environ gives way to the real look of the country – well-kept and smiling still, but tranquil and sweetly shaded, with big farmyards, quiet country lanes, and a quiet country look in the peasants' faces.

In passing through some parts of France one wonders where the inhabitants of the châteaux go when they emerge from their gates – so interminably, beyond those gates, do the flat fields, divided by straight unshaded roads, reach out to every point of the compass; but here the wooded undulations of the country, the friendliness of the villages, the recurrence of big rambling farmsteads – some, apparently, the remains of fortified monastic granges – all suggest the possibility of something resembling the English rural life, with its traditional ties between park and fields.

The brief journey between Versailles and Fontainebleau offers – if one takes the longer way, by Saint Rémy-les-Chevreuse and Etampes – a succession of charming impressions, more varied than one often finds in a long day's motor-run through France; and midway one comes upon the splendid surprise of Dourdan.

Ignorance is not without its æsthetic uses; and to drop down into the modest old town without knowing – or having forgotten, if one prefers to put it so – the great castle of Philip

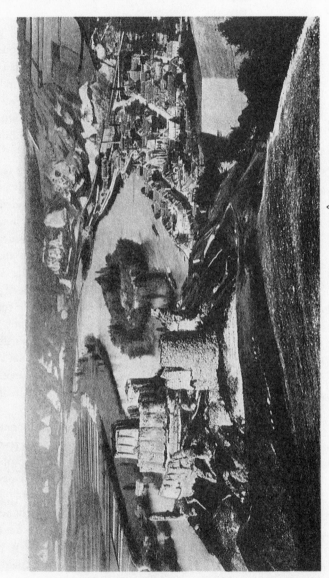

LE PETIT ANDELY: VIEW OF THE TOWN AND CHÂTEAU GAILLARD

Augustus, which, moated, dungeoned, ivy-walled, still possesses its peaceful central square – to come on this vigorous bit of mediæval arrogance, with the little houses of Dourdan still ducking their humble roofs to it in an obsequious circle – well! to taste the full flavour of such sensations, it is worth while to be of a country where the last new grain-elevator or office building is the only monument that receives homage from the surrounding architecture.

Dourdan, too, has the crowning charm of an old inn facing its *château-fort* – such an inn as Manon and des Grieux dined in on the way to Paris – where, in a large courtyard shaded by trees, one may feast on strawberries and cheese at a table enclosed in clipped shrubs, with dogs and pigeons amicably prowling for crumbs, and the host and hostess, their maid-servants, ostlers and *marmitons* breakfasting at another long table, just across the hedge. Now that the demands of the motorist are introducing modern plumbing and Maple furniture into the uttermost parts of France, these romantic old inns, where it is charming to breakfast, if precarious to sleep, are becoming as rare as the mediæval keeps with which they are, in a way, contemporaneous; and Dourdan is fortunate in still having two such perfect specimens to attract the attention of the archæologist.

Etampes, our next considerable town, seemed by contrast rather featureless and disappointing; yet, for that very reason, so typical of the average French country town – dry, compact, unsentimental, as if avariciously hoarding a long rich past – that its one straight grey street and squat old church will hereafter always serve for the *ville de province* background in my staging of French fiction. Beyond Etampes, as one approaches Fontainebleau, the scenery grows extremely picturesque, with bold outcroppings of blackened rock, fields of golden broom, groves of birch and pine – first hints of the fantastic sandstone scenery of the forest. And presently the long green aisles opened before us in all the freshness of spring verdure – tapering away right and left to distant *ronds-points*, to mossy stone crosses and obelisks – and leading us toward sunset to the old town in the heart of the forest.

Four
THE LOIRE AND THE INDRE

FONTAINEBLEAU IS CHARMING in May, and at no season do its glades more invitingly detain the wanderer; but it belonged to the familiar, the already-experienced part of our itinerary, and we had to press on to the unexplored. So after a day's roaming of the forest, and a short flight to Moret, mediævally seated in its stout walls on the poplar-edged Loing, we started on our way to the Loire.

Here, too, our wheels were still on beaten tracks; though the morning's flight across country to Orléans was meant to give us a glimpse of a new region. But on that unhappy morning Boreas was up with all his pack, and hunted us savagely across the naked plain, now behind, now on our quarter, now dashing ahead to lie in ambush behind a huddled village, and leap on us as we rounded its last house. The plain stretched on interminably, and the farther it stretched the harder the wind raced us; so that Pithiviers, spite of dulcet associations, appeared to our shrinking eyes only as a wind-break, eagerly striven for and too soon gained and passed; and when, at luncheon-time, we beat our way, spent and wheezing, into Orléans, even the serried memories of that venerable city endeared it to us less than the fact that it had an inn where we might at last find shelter.

The above wholly inadequate description of an interesting part of France will have convinced any rational being that motoring is no way to see the country. And that morning it certainly was not; but then, what of the afternoon? When we rolled out of Orléans after luncheon, both the day and the scene had changed; and what other form of travel could have brought us into such communion with the spirit of the Loire as our smooth flight along its banks in the bland May air? For, after all, if the motorist sometimes misses details by going too fast, he sometimes has them stamped into his memory by an opportune puncture or a recalcitrant 'magneto'; and if, on windy days, he has to rush through nature blindfold, on golden afternoons such as this he can drain every drop of her precious essence.

Certainly we got a great deal of the Loire as we followed its windings that day: a great sense of the steely breadth of its flow, the amenity of its shores, the sweet flatness of the richly gardened and vineyarded landscape, as of a highly cultivated but slightly insipid society; an impression of long white villages and of stout conical towns on little hills; of old brown Beaugency in its cup between two heights, and Madame de Pompadour's Ménars on its bright terraces; of Blois, nobly bestriding the river at a noble bend; and farther south, of yellow cliffs honeycombed with strange dwellings; of Chaumont and Amboise crowning their heaped-up towns; of *manoirs*, walled gardens, rich pastures, willowed islands; and then, toward sunset, of another long bridge, a brace of fretted church-towers, and the widespread roofs of Tours.

Had we visited by rail the principal places named in this itinerary, necessity would have detained us longer in each, and we should have had a fuller store of specific impressions; but we should have missed what is, in one way, the truest initiation of travel, the sense of continuity, of relation between different districts, of familiarity with the unnamed, unhistoried region stretching between successive centres of human history, and exerting, in deep unnoticed ways, so persistent an influence on the turn that history takes. And after all – though some people seem to doubt the fact – it is possible to stop a motor and get out of it; and if, on our way down the Loire, we exercised this privilege infrequently, it was because, here again, we were in a land of old acquaintance, of which the general topography was just the least familiar part.

It was not till, two days later, we passed out of Tours – not, in fact, till we left to the northward the towered pile of Loches – that we found ourselves once more in a new country. It was a cold day of high clouds and flying sunlight: just the sky to overarch the wide rolling landscape through which the turns of the Indre were leading us. To the south, whither we were bound, lay the Berry – the land of George Sand; while to the north-west low acclivities sloped away, with villages shining on their sides. One arrow of sunlight, I remember, transfixed for a second an unknown town on one of these slopes: a town of some consequence, with walls and towers that flashed far-off and mysterious across the cloudy plain. Who has not been tantalized in travelling, by the glimpse of such cities – unnamed, undiscoverable afterward by the minutest orientations of map and guide-book? Certainly, to the uninitiated, no hill-town is visible on that particularly level section of the map of France; yet there sloped the hill, there shone the town – not a moment's mirage, but the companion of an hour's travel, dominating the turns of our road, beckoning to us across the increasing miles, and causing me to vow, as we lost the last glimpse of its towers, that next year I would go back and make it give up its name.

But now we were approaching a town with a name – a name so encrusted and overgrown with associations that it was undeniably disappointing, as we reached its outskirts, to find

ORLÉANS: GENERAL VIEW OF THE TOWN

Châteauroux – aside from its fine old château on the Indre – so exactly like other dull French towns, so provokingly unconscious of being one of the capital cities of literature. And it seems, in fact, literally as well as figuratively unaware of its distinction. Fame throws its circles so wide that it makes not a ripple near home; and even the alert landlady of the Hôtel Sainte Catherine wrinkled her brows perplexedly at our question: 'Is one permitted to visit the house of George Sand?'

'*Le château de George Sand?* (A pause of reflection.) *C'est l'écrivain, n'est-ce pas?* (Another pause.) *C'est à Nohant, le château? Mais, Madame, je ne saurais vous le dire.*'

Yet here was the northern gate of the Sand country – it was here that, for years, the leaders of the most sedentary profession of a sedentary race – the *hommes de lettres* of France – descended from the Paris express, and took a diligence on their pilgrimage to the oracle. When one considers the fatigue of the long day's railway journey, and the French dread of *déplacements*, the continual stream of greatness that Paris poured out upon Nohant gives the measure of what Nohant had to offer in return.

As we sat at breakfast in the inn dining-room we irreverently pictured some of these great personages – Liszt, Sainte-Beuve, Gautier, Dumas fils, Flaubert – illustrious figures in the queer dishabille of travel, unwinding strange *cache-nez*, solicitous for embroidered carpet-bags, seated in that very room over their coffee and omelette, or climbing to the coupé of the diligence outside. And then we set out on the same road.

Straight as an arrow, after the unvarying fashion of the French government highway, it runs south-east through vast wheatfields, past barns and farmhouses grouped as in the vanished 'drawing-books' of infancy – now touching, now deserting the Indre banks, as the capricious river throws its poplar-edged loops across the plain. But presently we began to mount insensibly; till at length a sharp turn, and an abrupt fall of the land, brought us out on a ridge above the plain of the Berry, with the river reappearing below, and far, far south a blue haze of mountains.

The road, after that, descends again by gentle curves, acquainting one gradually with the charming details of the foreground – pale-green copses, fields hedged with hawthorn, long lines of poplars in the plain – while, all the way, the distant horizon grows richer, bluer and more mysterious. It is a wide lonely country, with infrequent villages – mere hamlets – dotting the fields; one sees how the convivial Dudevant, coming from the livelier Gascony, might have found it, for purposes of pot-house sociability, a little thinly settled. At one of these small lonely villages – Vicq – just where the view spreads widest, the road loses it again by a gradual descent of a mile or so; and at the foot of the hill, among hawthorn and lilac hedges, through the boughs of budding trees, a high slate roof shows to the left – the roof of a plain-faced fawn-coloured house, the typical *gentilhommière* of the French countryside.

No other house is in sight: only, from behind the trees, peep two or three humble tiled cottages, dependencies of the larger pile. There is nothing to tell us the name of the house – nothing to signalize it, to take it out of the common. It stands there large, placid, familiarly related to the high-road and the farm, like one side of the extraordinary woman it sheltered; and perhaps that fact helps to suggest its name, to render almost superfluous our breathless question to the pretty goose-girl knitting under the hedge.

'*Mais oui, Madame – c'est Nohant.*'

The goose-girl – pink as a hawthorn bud, a 'kerchief' tied about her curls – might really, in the classic phrase of sentimental travel, have 'stepped out' of one of the novels written yonder, under the high roof to which she pointed: she had the honest savour of the *terroir*, yet with that superadded grace that the author of the novels has been criticized for bestowing on her peasants. She formed, at any rate, a charming link between our imagination and the famous house; and we presently found that the miracle which had preserved her in all her 1830 grace had been extended to the whole privileged spot, which seemed, under a clear glass bell of oblivion, to have been kept intact, unchanged, like some wonderful 'exhibit' illustrative of the extraordinary history lived within it.

The house faces diagonally toward the road, from which a high wall once screened it; but it is written in the *Histoire de ma vie* that M. Dudevant, in a burst of misdirected activity, threw down several yards of this wall, and filled the opening with a hedge. The hedge is still there; and thanks to this impulse of destruction, the traveller obtains a glimpse of grass terraces and stone steps, set in overgrown thickets of lilac, hawthorn and acacia, and surmounted by the long tranquil front of the château. On each side, beyond the stretch of hedge, the wall begins again; terminating, at one corner of the property, in a massive old cow-stable with a round pepperpot tower; at the opposite end is a charming conical-roofed garden-pavilion, with mossy steps ascending to it from the road.

At right angles to the highway, a shady lane leads down past the farm buildings; and following this, one comes, around their flank, on a large pleasant untidy farmyard, full of cows and chickens, and divided by the long range of the *communs* from the entrance-court of the château. Farmyard and court

NOHANT: CHÂTEAU OF GEORGE SAND

both face on a small grassy place – what, in England, would pass for a diminutive common – in the centre of which, under an ancient walnut tree, stands a much more ancient church – a church so tiny, black and shrunken that it somehow suggests a blind old peasant woman mumbling and dozing in the shade. This is the parish church of Nohant; and a few yards from it, adjoining the court of the château, lies the little walled graveyard which figures so often in the *Histoire de ma vie*, and where she who described it now rests with her kin. The graveyard is defended from intrusion by a high wall and a locked gate; and after all her spirit is not there, but in the house and the garden – above all, in the little cluster of humble old cottages enclosing the shady place about the church, and constituting, apparently, the whole village of Nohant. Like the goose-girl, these little houses are surprisingly picturesque and sentimental; and their mossy roofs, their clipped yews, the old white-capped women who sit spinning on their doorsteps, supply almost too ideal an answer to one's hopes.

And when, at last, excitedly and enchantedly, one has taken in the quiet perfection of it all, and turned to confront the great question: Does a sight of Nohant deepen the mystery, or elucidate it? – one can only answer, in the cautious speech of the New England casuist: *Both*. For if it helps one to understand one side of George Sand's life, it seems actually to cast a thicker obscurity over others – even if, among the different sides contemplated, one includes only those directly connected with the place, and not the innumerable facets that reflected Paris, Venice, Fontainebleau and Majorca.

The first surprise is to find the place, on the whole, so much more – shall one say? – dignified and decent, so much more conscious of social order and restraints, than the early

NOHANT: GARDEN PAVILION

years of the life led in it. The pictures of Nohant in the *Histoire de ma vie* are unlike any other description of French provincial manners at that period, suggesting rather an affinity with the sombre Brontë background than the humdrum but conventional and orderly existence of the French rural gentry.

When one recalls the throng of motley characters who streamed in and out of that quiet house – the illegitimate children of both sides, living in harmony with one another and with the child of wedlock, the too-intimate servants, the peasant playmates, the drunken boon companions – when one turns to the Hogarthian pictures of midnight carouses presided over by the uproarious Hippolyte and the sombrely tippling Dudevant, while their wives sat disgusted, but apparently tolerant, above stairs, one feels one's self in the sinister gloom of Wildfell Hall rather than in the light temperate air of a French province. And somehow, unreasonably of course, one expects the house to bear, even outwardly, some mark of that dark disordered period – or, if not, then of the cheerful but equally incoherent and inconceivable existence led there when the timid Madame Dudevant was turning into the great George Sand, and the strange procession which continued to stream through the house was composed no longer of drunken gentlemen-farmers and left-handed peasant relations, but of an almost equally fantastic and ill-assorted company of ex-priests, naturalists, journalists, Saint-Simonians, riders of every conceivable religious, political and literary hobby, among whom the successive tutors of the adored Maurice – forming in themselves a line as long as the kings in *Macbeth*! – perhaps take the palm for oddness of origin and adaptability of manners.

One expected the scene of these confused and incessant comings and goings to wear the injured *déclassé* air of a house which has never had its rights respected – a house long accustomed to jangle its dinner-bell in vain and swing its broken hinges unheeded; and instead, one beholds this image of aristocratic well-being, this sober edifice, conscious in every line of its place in the social scale, of its obligations to the church and cottages under its wing, its rights over the acres surrounding it. And so one may, not too fancifully, recognize in it the image of those grave ideals to which George Sand gradually conformed the passionate experiment of her life; may even indulge one's self by imagining that an old house so marked in its very plainness, its conformity, must have exerted, over a mind as sensitive as hers, an unperceived but persistent influence, giving her that centralizing weight of association and habit which is too often lacking in modern character, and standing ever before her as the shrine of those household pieties to which, inconsistently enough, but none the less genuinely, the devotion of her last years was paid.

Five

NOHANT TO CLERMONT

THERE HAPPENED TO us, on leaving Nohant, what had happened after Beauvais: the quiet country house by the roadside, like the mighty Gothic choir, possessed our thoughts to the exclusion of other impressions. As far as La Châtre, indeed – the little town on the Indre, where young Madame Dudevant spent a winter to further her husband's political ambitions – we were still within the Nohant radius; and it was along the straight road we were travelling that poor old Madame Dupin de Francueil – *si douillette* that she could hardly make the round of the garden – fled in her high-heeled slippers on the fatal night when her son, returning from a gay supper at La Châtre, was flung from his horse and killed at the entrance to the town. These scenes from the *Histoire de ma vie* are so vivid, they live so poignantly in memory, that in reliving them on the spot one feels, with Goncourt, how great their writer would have been had her intrepid pen more often remained *dans le vrai*.

La Châtre is a charming town, with a remarkably picturesque approach, on the Nohant side, across an old bridge out of which an old house, with a steep terraced garden, seems to grow with the conscious pleasure of well-grouped masonry: and the streets beyond have an air of ripe experience tempered by gaiety, like that of those ironic old eighteenth-century faces wherein the wrinkles are as gay as dimples.

Southward from La Châtre, the road runs through a

beautiful hilly country to Montluçon on the Cher: a fine old border town, with a brave fighting past, and interesting relics of Bourbon ascendancy; but now deeply disfigured by hideous factories and long grimy streets of operatives' houses. In deploring the ravages of modern industry on one of these rare old towns, it is hard to remember that they are not museum pieces, but settlements of human beings with all the normal desire to prosper at whatever cost to the physiognomy of their birthplace; and Montluçon in especial seems to have been a very pelican to the greed of her offspring.

We had meant to spend the night there, but there was a grimness about the inn – the special grimness of which the commercial travellers' hotel in the French manufacturing town holds the depressing secret – that forbade even a glance at the bedrooms; and though it was near sunset we pressed on for Vichy. We had, in consequence, but a cold twilight glimpse of the fine gorge of Montaigut, through which the road cuts its way to Gannat, the first town to the north of the Limagne; and night had set in when we traversed the plain of the Allier. On good French roads, however, a motor-journey by night is not without its compensations; and our dark flight through mysterious fields and woods terminated, effectively enough, with the long descent down a lamp-garlanded boulevard into the inanimate white watering-place.

Vichy, in fact, had barely opened the shutters of its fashionable hotels: the season does not begin till June, and in May only a few premature bathers – mostly English – shiver in corners of the marble halls, or disconsolately peruse last year's news in the deserted reading-rooms. But even in this semi-chrysalis stage the town presented itself, the next morning, as that rarest of spectacles – grace triumphant over the processes of the toilet. Only a pretty woman and a French *ville*

CLERMONT–FERRAND: NOTRE–DAME DU PORT

d'eau can look really charming in morning dishabille; and the way in which Vichy accomplishes the feat would be a lesson to many pretty women.

The place, at all seasons, is an object-lesson to less enlightened municipalities; and when one finds one's self vainly wishing that art and history, and all the rich tapestry of the past, might somehow be brought before the eyes of our self-sufficient millions, one might pause to ask if the sight of a well-kept, self-respecting French town, carefully and artistically planned as a setting to the amenities of life, would not, after all, offer the more salutary and surprising example.

Vichy, even among French towns, stands out as a singularly finished specimen of what such municipal pride can accomplish. From its broad plane-shaded *promenade*, flanked by bright-faced hotels, and by the arcades of the Casino, to the park on the Allier, and the wide circumjacent boulevards, it wears, at every turn, the same trim holiday air, the rouge and patches of smooth gravel, bright flower-borders, gay shops, shady benches, inviting cafés. Even the cab-stands, with their smart vis-à-vis and victorias drawn by plump cobs in tinkling harnesses, seem part of a dream-town, where all that is usually sordid and shabby has been touched by the magic wand of trimness; or where some utopian millionaire has successfully demonstrated that the sordid and shabby need never exist at all.

But, to the American observer, Vichy is perhaps most instructive just because it is not the millionaire's wand which has worked the spell; because the town owes its gaiety and its elegance, not to the private villa, the rich man's 'showplace', but to wise public expenditure of the money which the bathers annually pour into its exchequer.

It was, however, rather for the sake of its surroundings than for the study of its unfolding season, that we had come there; and the neighbouring country offered the richest return for our enterprise.

From the plain of the Limagne the hills slope up behind Vichy in a succession of terraces divided by streams and deeply wooded glens, and connected by the interlacing of admirable roads that civilizes the remotest rural districts of France. Climbing these gradual heights to the hill-village of Ferrières, we had, the day after our arrival, our first initiation into what the near future held for us – a glorious vision, across the plain, of the Monts Dore and the Monts de Dôme. The blue mountain haze that had drawn us steadily southward, from our first glimpse of it on the heights of the Berry, now resolved itself into a range of wild volcanic forms, some curved like the bell-shaped apses of the churches of Auvergne, some slenderly cup-like, and showing the hollow rim of the spent crater; all fantastic, individual, indescribably differentiated in line and colour from mountain forms of less violent origin. And between them and us lay the richest contrasting landscape, the deep meadows and luxuriant woodlands of the Allier vale, with here and there a volcanic knoll lifting on its crest an old town or a Rhenish-looking castle. The landscape, thus viewed, presents a perplexing mixture of suggestions, recalling now the brown hill-villages of Umbria, now the robber castles of the Swiss Rhineland; with a hint, again, of the Terra di Lavore in its bare mountain lines, and the prodigal fertility of their lower slopes; so that one felt one's self moving in a confusion of scenes romantically combined, as in the foreground of a Claude or a Wilson, for the greater pleasure of the eclectic eye.

The only landscape that seems to have been excluded from the composition is that of France; all through Auvergne, we never felt ourselves in France. But that is, of course, merely because the traveller's France is apt to be mainly made up of bits of the Ile-de-France and Normandy and Brittany; and not till one has explored the central and south-western provinces does one learn of the countless Frances within France, and realize that one may find one's 'Switzerland, one's Italy' without crossing the Alps to reach them.

We had, the next day, a closer impression of the scene we had looked down on from Ferrières; motoring first along the high ridge above the Limagne to the ancient black hill-town of Thiers, and thence descending again to the plain. Our way led across it, by the charming castled town of Pont-de-Château, to Clermont-Ferrand, which spreads its swarthy mass at the base of the Puy de Dôme – that strangest, sternest of cities, all built and paved in the black volcanic stone of Volvic, and crowned by the sinister splendour of its black cathedral. It was Viollet-le-Duc who added the west front and towers to this high ancient pile; and for once his rash hand was so happily inspired that, at the first glimpse of his twin spires soaring above the roofs of Clermont, one forgives him – for the moment – the wrong he did to Blois, to Pierrefonds and Vézelay.

Six
IN AUVERGNE

A T LAST WE were really in Auvergne. On our balcony at
Royat, just under the flank of the Puy de Dôme, we
found ourselves in close communion with its tossed heights,
its black towns, its threatening castles. And Royat itself – even
the dull new watering-place quarter – is extremely characteristic of the region: hanging in a cleft of the great volcanic
upheaval, with hotels, villas, gardens, vineyards clutching
precariously at every ledge and fissure, as though just arrested
in their descent on the roofs of Clermont.

As a watering-place Royat is not an ornamental specimen
of its class; and it has the farther disadvantage of being
connected with Clermont by a long dusty suburb, noisy with
tram-cars; but as a centre for excursions it offers its good hotels
and 'modern conveniences' at the precise spot most favourable
to the motorist, who may radiate from it upon almost every
centre of interest in Auvergne, and return at night to digestible
food and clean beds – two requisites for which, in central
France, one is often doomed to pine.

Auvergne, one of the most interesting, and hitherto almost
the least known, of the old French provinces, offers two
distinct and equally striking sides to the appreciative traveller:
on the one hand, its remarkably individual church architecture, and on the other, the no less personal character of its
landscape. Almost all its towns are distinguished by one of
those ancient swarthy churches, with western narthex, great

central tower, and curious incrustations of polychrome lava, which marked, in Auvergne, as strongly distinctive an architectural impulse as flowered, on a vastly larger scale, and a century or more later, in the Gothic of the Ile de France. And the towns surrounding these churches, on the crest or flank of one of the volcanic eminences springing from the plain – the towns themselves, with their narrow perpendicular streets and tall black houses, are so darkly individual, so plainly akin to the fierce predatory castles on the neighbouring hills, that one is arrested at every turn by the desire to follow up the obscure threads of history connecting them with this little-known portion of the rich French past.

But to the traveller restricted by time, the other side of the picture – its background, rather, of tormented blue peaks and wide-spread forest – which must assert itself, at all seasons, quite as distinctively as the historic and architectural character of the towns, is likely, in May, to carry off the victory. We had come, at any rate, with the modest purpose of taking a mere bird's-eye view of the region, such a flight across the scene as draws one back, later, to brood and hover; and our sight of the landscape from the Royat balcony confirmed us in the resolve to throw as sweeping a glance as possible, and defer the study of details to our next – our already-projected! – visit.

The following morning, therefore, we set out early for the heart of the Monts Dore. Our road carried us southward, along a series of ridges above the wide Allier vale, and then up and down, over wild volcanic hills, now densely wooded, now desolately bare. We were on the road to Issoire and La Chaise Dieu, two of the most notable old towns of southern Auvergne; but, in pursuit of scenery, we reluctantly turned off at the village of Coudes, at the mouth of a lateral valley, and struck up toward the western passes which lead to the Pic de Sancy.

Some miles up this valley, which follows the capricious windings of the Couzes, lie the baths of Saint Nectaire-le-Bas, romantically planted in a narrow defile, beneath the pyramidal Romanesque church which the higher-lying original village lifts up on a steep splinter of rock. The landscape beyond Saint Nectaire grows more rugged and Alpine in character: the pastures have a Swiss look, and the shaggy mountain-sides are clothed with a northern growth of beech and pine. Presently, at a turn of the road, we came on the little crater-lake of Chambon, its vivid blueness set in the greenest of meadows, and overhung by the dark basalt cliff which carries on its summit the fortified castle of Murols. The situation of Murols, lifted on its shaft of rock above that lonely upland valley, is in itself impressive enough to bring out the full value of such romantic suggestions as it has to offer; and the monument is worthy of its site. It is in fact a very noble ruin, raising its central keep above two outer circuits of battered masonry, the ampler and later of which shows the classical pilasters and large fenestration of what must have been one of the stateliest specimens of the last stage of French feudal architecture. Though the guide-books record a mention of Murols as early as the thirteenth century, the castle now standing is all of later date, and the great rectangular exterior is an interesting example of the transitional period when Italian palace architecture began to be grafted on the rugged stock of French military construction.

Just beyond the lake of Chambon the road begins to mount the long curves of the Col de Diane, the pass which leads over into the valley of Mont Dore. As we rose through bleak meadows and patches of scant woodland, the mountains of

Auvergne unrolled themselves to the east in one of those lonely tossing expanses of summit and ridge and chasm that suggest the mysterious undulations of some uninhabited planet. Though the Col de Diane is not a high pass, it gives, from its yoke, a strangely memorable impression of distance and mystery; partly, perhaps, because in that desert region there is neither village nor house to break the labyrinth of peaks; but chiefly because of the convulsed outlines into which they have been tossed by subterranean fires.

A cold wind swept the top of the pass, and snow still lay under the rocks by the roadside; so that it was cheering to the spirits, as well as to the eye, when we presently began our descent through dark pine forests into the vale of the Dordogne. The baths of Mont Dore lie directly beneath the pass, at the mouth of a valley hollowed out of the side of the Pic de Sancy, the highest peak in Auvergne. In spite of milder air and bright spring foliage we were still distinctly in high places; and Mont Dore itself, not yet decked for the entertainment of its bathers, had the poverty-stricken look which everywhere marks the real mountain village. Later, no doubt, when its hotels are open, and its scanty gardens in bloom, it takes on a thin veneer of frivolity; but it must always be an austere-looking village, with its ill-kept cobblestone streets, and gaunt stone houses grouped against a background of Alpine pastures. We were not sorry, therefore, that its few restaurants presented barred shutters to our midday hunger, and that we were obliged to follow the first footsteps of the infant Dordogne down the valley to the lower-lying baths of Bourboule.

The Dordogne is a child of lusty growth, and at its very leap from the cradle, under the Pic de Sancy, it rolls a fine brown torrent beneath steeply wooded banks. Its course led us rapidly down the mountain glen to the amiable but somewhat characterless little watering-place of La Bourboule, set in a depression of the hills, with a background of slopes which, in summer, might offer fairly pleasant walks between one's douches; and here, at a fresh white hotel with an affable landlady, we lunched on trout that must have leapt straight from the Dordogne into the frying-pan.

After luncheon we once more took our way along the lively curves of the river; to part with them at last, reluctantly, a few miles down the valley, and strike out across a dull plateau to the mountain town of Laqueille – a gaunt wind-beaten place, with nothing of note to offer except its splendid view from the dizzy verge of a high cornice which overhangs the valley running south from the chain of the Dôme. Beyond Laqueille, again, we began to descend by long windings; and at last, turning off from the direct road to Royat, we engaged ourselves in a series of wooded gorges, in search of the remote village of Orcival.

The church of Orcival is one of the most noted of that strange group of Auvergnat churches which some students of French Romanesque are disposed to attribute, not only to one brief period of time, but to the hand of one architect; so closely are they allied, not alone in plan and construction, but in their peculiar and original decorative details. We had resolved, therefore, not to return to Royat without a sight of Orcival; and spite of the misleading directions plentifully bestowed on us by the way, and resulting in endless doublings through narrow lonely glens, we finally came, in the neck of the last and narrowest, upon a huddled group of stone roofs with a church rising nobly above them.

Here it was at last – and our first glance told us how well worth the search we had made for it. But a second made evident the disturbing fact that a cattle-fair was going on in the

ORCIVAL: THE CHURCH

village; and though this is not an unusual event in French towns, or one calculated, in general, to interfere with the movements of the sightseer, we soon saw that, owing to the peculiar position of Orcival, which is jammed into the head of its glen as tightly as a cork in a bottle, the occupation of the square about the church formed a complete check to circulation.

And the square was fully occupied: it presented, as we descended on it, an agitated surface of blue human backs, and dun and white bovine ones, so closely and inextricably mixed that any impact from without merely sent a wave across the mass, without making the slightest break in its substance. On its edge, therefore, we halted; the church, with its beautiful rounded *chevet* and central pyramid tower, islanded a few yards away across a horned sea which divided it from us as hopelessly as Egypt from Israel; and the waves of the sea setting toward us with somewhat threatening intent at the least sign of our attempting to cross it. There was therefore nothing to be done but to own ourselves intruders, and defer a sight of Orcival till our next visit; and with much backing and wriggling, and some unfavourable comment on the part of the opposition, we effected a crestfallen exit from that interesting but inhospitable village.

The road thence to Royat climbs over the long Col de Ceyssat, close under the southern side of the Puy de Dôme, and we looked up longingly at the bare top of the mountain, yearning to try the ascent, but fearing that our 'horse-power' was not pitched to such heights. That adventure too was therefore deferred till our next visit, which every renunciation of the kind was helping to bring nearer and make more inevitable; and we pushed on to Royat across the plain of Laschamp, noted in the records of motoring as the starting-point of the perilous *circuit d'Auvergne*.

Seven

ROYAT TO BOURGES

T HE TERM OF our holiday was upon us and, stern necessity took us back, the next day, to Vichy. We followed, this time, the road along the western side of the Limagne, passing through the old towns of Riom and Aigueperse. Riom, thanks to its broad boulevards and bright open squares, struck us as the most cheerful and animated place we had seen in Auvergne; and it has, besides, a great air of Renaissance elegance, many of its old traceried hôtels having been built in the sixteenth century, which saw the chief development of the town.

Aigueperse, on the contrary, in spite of its situation in the same sunny luxuriant plain, presents the morose aspect of the typical town of Auvergne, without many compensating merits, save that of two striking pictures of the Italian school which are to be seen in its modernized cathedral. From Aigueperse our road struck eastward across the Limagne to Gannat; and thence, through pleasant fields and woods, we returned to Vichy, on the opposite edge of the plain.

We started early the next morning on our journey to the north, for our slight experience of the inns of central France made us anxious to reach Orléans by night. Such long runs cannot be made without the sacrifice of much that charms and arrests one by the way; and this part of the country should be seen at leisure, in the long summer days, when the hotels are less sepulchrally damp, and when one can remain late out of

71

doors, instead of having to shiver through the evening hours around a smoky oil-lamp, in a room which will not bear inspection even by that inadequate light.

We suffered, I remember, many pangs by the way; and not least, that of having to take as a mere parenthesis the charmingly complete little town of La Palisse on the Bèbre, with the ruined ivied castle of the Comtes de Chabannes overhanging a curve of the river, and grouping itself in a memorable composition with the picturesque houses below it.

Farther north, again, Moulins on the Allier inflicted a still deeper pang; for this fine old town has considerable claims to distinction besides the great triptych that made its name known through Europe after the recent exhibition of French Primitives in Paris. The Virgin of Moulins, gloriously enthroned in the cathedral among her soft-faced Lombard angels, remains undoubtedly the crowning ornament of the town, if only on account of the problem which she holds out, so inscrutably, to explorers of the baffling annals of early French art. But aside from this pre-eminent possession, and the interest of several minor relics, Moulins has the attraction of its own amiable and distinguished physiognomy. With its streets of light-coloured stone, its handsome eighteenth-century hôtels and broad well-paved *cours*, it seemed, after the grim black towns of the south, a singularly open and cheerful place; and one was conscious, behind the handsome stone gateways and balconied façades, of the existence of old panelled drawing-rooms with pastel portraits and faded tapestry furniture.

The approach to Nevers, the old capital of the Nivernais, carried us abruptly back to the Middle Ages, but to an exuberant northern mediævalism far removed from the Gallo-Roman tradition of central France. The cathedral of Nevers, with its ornate portals and fantastically decorated clock-tower, has, in the old ducal palace across the square, a rival more than capable of meeting its challenge on equal grounds: a building of really gallant exterior, with fine angle towers, and within, a great staircase commemorating in luxuriant sculpture the legendary beginnings of that ancient house of Cleves which, in the fifteenth century, allied itself by marriage with the dukes of Burgundy.

At Nevers we found ourselves once more on the Loire; but only to break from it again in a long dash across country to Bourges. At this point we left behind us the charming diversified scenery which had accompanied us to the borders of the Loire, and entered on a region of low monotonous undulations, flattening out gradually into the vast wheat-fields about Bourges. But who would wish any other setting for that memorable silhouette, throned, from whichever point of the compass one approaches it, in such proud isolation above the plain? One forgets even, in a distant view of Bourges, that nature has helped, by an opportune rise of the ground, to lift the cathedral to its singular eminence: the hill, and the town upon it, seem so merely the unremarked pedestal of the monument. It is not till one climbs the steep street leading up from the Place Saint Bonnet that one realizes the peculiar topographical advantages of such a site; advantages which perhaps partly account for the overwhelming and not quite explicable effect of a first sight of the cathedral.

Even now, on a second visit, with the great monuments of the Ile de France fresh in memory, we felt the same effect, and the same difficulty in running it down, in differentiating it from the richer, yet perhaps less deeply Gothic impression produced by the rival churches of the north. For, begin as one will by admitting, by insisting upon, the defects of Bourges –

MOULINS: PLACE DE L'HÔTEL-DE-VILLE AND THE JACQUEMART TOWER

its irregular inharmonious façade, its thin piers, its mean outer aisles – one yet ends in a state where criticism perforce yields to sensation, where one surrenders one's self wholly to the spell of its spiritual suggestion. Certainly it would be hard to put a finger, either within or without, on the specific tangible cause of this feeling. Is it to be found in the extraordinary beauty of the five western portals, so crowded with noble and pathetic imagery and delicate ornamental detail? But the doors of Chartres surpass even these! Is it then, if one looks within, the rich blue and red of its dense ancient glass? But Chartres, again, has finer glass of that unmatched period. Is it the long clear sweep of the nave and aisles, uninterrupted by the cross-lines of transept or chancel-screen? But if one recalls the wonderful convolutions of the ambulatory of Canterbury, one has to confess that Gothic art – even in its conventionalized English form – has created curves of greater poetry and mystery, produced a more thrilling sense of shadowy conse-crated distances. Perhaps the spell of Bourges resides in a fortunate accidental mingling of many of the qualities that predominate in this or that more perfect structure – in the mixing of the ingredients so that there rises from them, as one stands in one of the lofty inner aisles, with one's face toward the choir, that breath of mystical devotion which issues from the very heart of mediæval Christianity.

'With this sweetness,' wrote Saint Theresa, of the Prayer of Quiet, 'the whole inner and outer man seems to be delighted, as though some delicious ointment were poured into the soul like an exquisite perfume ... as if we suddenly came to a place where it is exhaled, not only from one, but from many things; and we know not what it is, or from which one of them it comes, but they all penetrate us ...' If Amiens, in its harmony of conception and vigour of execution, seems to embody the developing will power of a people passionate in belief, and indomitable in the concrete expression of their creed, here at Bourges one feels that other, less expressible side of the great ruling influence of the Middle Ages – the power that willed mighty monuments and built them, yet also, even in its moments of most brutal material ascendancy, created the other houses, not built with hands, where the spirits of the saints might dwell.

PART TWO

One

PARIS TO POITIERS

S PRING AGAIN, AND the long white road unrolling itself southward from Paris. How could one resist the call?

We answered it on the blandest of late March mornings, all April in the air, and the Seine fringing itself with a mist of yellowish willows as we rose over it, climbing the hill to Ville d'Avray. Spring comes soberly, inaudibly as it were, in these temperate European lands, where the grass holds its green all winter, and the foliage of ivy, laurel, holly, and countless other evergreen shrubs, links the lifeless to the living months. But the mere act of climbing that southern road above the Seine meadows seemed as definite as the turning of a leaf – the passing from a black-and-white page to one illuminated. And every day now would turn a brighter page for us.

Goethe has a charming verse, descriptive, it is supposed, of his first meeting with Christiane Vulpius: 'Aimlessly I strayed through the wood, *having it in my mind to seek nothing.*'

Such, precisely, was our state of mind on that first day's run. We were simply pushing south toward the Berry, through a more or less familiar country, and the real journey was to begin for us on the morrow, with the run from Châteauroux to Poitiers. But we reckoned without our France! It is easy enough, glancing down the long page of the *Guide Continental*, to slip by such names as Versailles, Rambouillet, Chartres and Valençay, in one's dash for the objective point; but there is no slipping by them in the motor, they lurk there in one's path, throwing out great loops of persuasion, arresting one's flight, complicating one's impressions, oppressing, bewildering one with the renewed, half-forgotten sense of the hoarded richness of France.

Versailles first, unfolding the pillared expanse of its north façade to vast empty perspectives of radiating avenues; then Rambouillet, low in a damp little park, with statues along green canals, and a look, this moist March weather, of being somewhat below sea level; then Maintenon, its rich red-purple walls and delicate stone ornament reflected in the moat dividing it from the village street. Both Rambouillet and Maintenon are characteristically French in their way of keeping company with their villages. Rambouillet, indeed, is slightly screened by a tall gate, a wall and trees; but Maintenon's warm red turrets look across the moat, straight into the windows of the opposite houses, with the simple familiarity of a time when class distinctions were too fixed to need emphasizing.

Our third château, Valençay – which, for comparison's sake, one may couple with the others though it lies far south of Blois – Valençay bears itself with greater aloofness, bidding the town 'keep its distance' down the hill on which the great house lifts its heavy angle-towers and flattened domes. A huge cliff-like wall, enclosing the whole southern flank of the hill, supports the terraced gardens before the château, which to the north is divided from the road by a vast *cour d'honneur* with a monumental grille and gateway. The impression is grander yet less noble.

But France is never long content to repeat her effects; and between Maintenon and Valençay she puts Chartres and Blois. Ah, these grey old cathedral towns with their narrow clean streets widening to a central *place* – at Chartres a beautiful oval, like the market-place in an eighteenth-century print – with

BOURGES: APSE OF THE CATHEDRAL

CHÂTEAU DE MAINTENON

their clipped lime-walks, high garden walls, Balzacian gables looking out on sunless lanes under the flanks of the granite giant! Save in the church itself, how frugally all the effects are produced – with how sober a use of greys and blacks, and pale high lights, as in some Van der Meer interior; yet how intense a suggestion of thrifty compact traditional life one gets from the low house-fronts, the barred gates, the glimpses of clean bare courts, the calm yet quick faces in the doorways! From these faces again one gets the same impression of remarkable effects produced by the discreetest means. The French physiognomy if not vividly beautiful is vividly intelligent; but the long practice of manners has so veiled its keenness with refinement as to produce a blending of vivacity and good temper nowhere else to be matched. And in looking at it one feels once more, as one so often feels in trying to estimate French architecture or the French landscape, how much of her total effect France achieves by elimination. If marked beauty be absent from the French face, how much more is marked dullness, marked brutality, the lumpishness of the clumsily made and the unfinished! As a mere piece of workmanship, of finish, the French provincial face – the peasant's face, even – often has the same kind of interest as a work of art.

One gets, after repeated visits to the 'show' towns of France, to feel these minor characteristics, the incidental graces of the foreground, almost to the exclusion of the great official spectacle in the centre of the picture; so that while the first image of Bourges or Chartres is that of a cathedral surrounded by a blur, later memories of the same places present a vividly individual town, with doorways, street corners, faces intensely remembered, and in the centre a great cloudy Gothic splendour.

At Chartres the cloudy splendour is shot through with such effulgence of colour that its vision, evoked by memory, seems to beat with a fiery life of its own, as though red blood ran in its stone veins. It is this suffusion of heat and radiance that chiefly, to the untechnical, distinguishes it from the other great Gothic interiors. In all the rest, colour, if it exists at all, burns in scattered unquiet patches, between wastes of shadowy grey stone and the wan pallor of later painted glass; but at Chartres those quivering waves of unearthly red and blue flow into and repeat each other in rivers of light, from their source in the great western rose, down the length of the vast aisles and clerestory, till they are gathered up at last into the mystical heart of the apse.

A short afternoon's run carried us through dullish country from Chartres to Blois, which we reached at the fortunate hour when sunset burnishes the great curves of the Loire and lays a plum-coloured bloom on the slate roofs overlapping, scale-like, the slope below the castle. There are few finer *roof-views* than this from the wall at Blois: the blue sweep of gables and ridge-lines billowing up here and there into a church tower with its *docheton* mailed in slate, or breaking to let through the glimpse of a carved façade, or the blossoming depths of a hanging garden; but perhaps only the eye subdued to tin house-tops and iron chimney-pots can feel the full poetry of old roofs.

Coming back to the Berry six weeks earlier than on our last year's visit, we saw how much its wide landscape needs the relief and modelling given by the varied foliage of May. Between bare woods and scarcely budded hedges the great meadows looked bleak and monotonous; and only the village gardens hung out a visible promise of spring. But in the sheltered enclosure at Nohant, spring seemed much nearer; at hand already in clumps of snowdrops and violets loosening the soil, in young red leaves on the rose-standards, and the twitter of birds in the heavy black-fruited ivy of the graveyard wall. A gate leads from the garden into the corner of the graveyard where George Sand and her children lie under an ancient yew. Feudal even in burial, they are walled off from the village dead, and the tombstone of Maurice Sand, as well as the monstrous stone chest over his mother's grave, bears the name of Dudevant and asserts a claim to the barony. Strange inconsequence of human desires, that the woman who had made her pseudonym illustrious enough to have it assumed by her whole family should cling in death to the obscure name of a repudiated husband; more inconsequent still that the descendant of kings, and the priestess of democracy and Fourierism, should insist on a right to the petty title which was never hers, since it was never Dudevant's to give! On the whole, the gravestones at Nohant are disillusioning; except indeed that of the wretched Solange, with its four tragic words: *La mère de Jeanne*.

But the real meaning of the place must be sought close by, behind the row of tall windows opening on the tangled mossy garden. They lead, these windows, straight into the life of George Sand: into the big cool dining-room, with its flagged floor and simple white-panelled walls, and the *salon* adjoining: the *salon*, alas, so radically remodelled in the unhappy mid-century period of wallpapers, stuffed furniture and centre table, that one seeks in vain for a trace of the original châtelaine of Nohant – that high-spirited, high-heeled old Madame Dupin who still haunts the panelled dining-room and the box-edged garden. Yet the *salon* has its special story to tell, for in George Sand's culminating time just such a long table with fringed cover and encircling armchairs formed the centre of French indoor life. About this elongated board sat the great woman's illustrious visitors, prolonging, as at a mental *table d'hôte*, that interminable dinner-talk which still strikes the hurried Anglo-Saxon as the typical expression of French sociability; and here the different arts of the household were practised – the painting, carving and fine needlework which a stronger-eyed generation managed to carry on by the light of a single lamp. Here, one likes especially to fancy, Maurice Sand exercised his chisel on the famous marionettes for the little theatre, while his mother, fitting their costumes with skilful fingers, listened, silent *comme une bête*, to the dissertations of Gautier, Flaubert or Dumas. The earlier life of the house still speaks, moreover, from the walls of the drawing-room, with the voice of jealously treasured ancestral portraits – pictures of the demoiselles Verrières, of the great Marshal and the beautiful Aurora – strange memorials of a past which explains so much in the history of George Sand, even to the tempestuous face of Solange Clésinger, looking darkly across the room at her simpering unremorseful progenitors.

Our guide, a close-capped brown-and-ruddy *bonne*, led us next, by circuitous passages, to the most interesting corner of the house: the little theatre contrived with artless ingenuity out of what might have been a store-room or wine-cellar. One should rather say the little theatres, however, for the mistress of revels had managed to crowd two stages into the limited space at her disposal; one, to the left, an actual *scène*, with 'life-size' scenery for real actors, the other, facing the entrance-door, the more celebrated marionette theatre, raised a few feet from the floor, with miniature proscenium arch and curtain; just such a *Puppen-theatre* as Wilhelm Meister described to Marianne, with a prolixity which caused that amiable but flighty young woman to fall asleep.

Between the two stages about twenty spectators might have found seats behind the front row of hard wooden benches reserved for the châtelaine and her most distinguished guests. A clean emptiness now pervades this temple of the arts: an emptiness made actually pathetic by the presence, on shelves at the back of the room, of the whole troupe of marionettes, brushed, spotless, well cared-for, and waiting only a touch on their wires to spring into life and populate their little stage. There they stand in wistful rows, the duenna, the Chimène, the *grande coquette*, Pantaloon, Columbine and Harlequin, Neapolitan fishers, odalisques and peasants, brigands and soldiers of the guard; all carved with a certain rude vivacity, and dressed, ingeniously and thriftily, by the indefatigable fingers which drove the quill all night upstairs.

It brought one close to that strange unfathomable life, which only at Nohant grows clear, shows bottom, as it were; closer still to be told by the red-brown *bonne* that 'Monsieur Maurice' had modelled many of his humorous peasant-types on '*les gens du pays*'; closest of all when she added, in answer to a question as to whether Madame Sand had really made the little frocks herself: 'Oh, yes, I remember seeing her at work on them, and helping her with it. I was twelve years old when she died.'

Here, then, was an actual bit of the Nohant tradition, before us in robust and lively middle age: one of the *berrichonnes* whom George Sand loved and celebrated, and who loved and served her in return. For a moment it brought Nohant within touch; yet the final effect of the contact, as one reflected on the vanished enthusiasms and ideals that George Sand's name revives, was the sense that the world of beliefs and ideas has seldom travelled so fast and far as in the years between 'Indiana' and today.

*

NEUVY–SAINT–SÉPULCRE: CHURCH OF THE PRECIOUS BLOOD

From La Châtre, just south of Nohant, we turned due west along the valley of the Creuse, through a country possessing some local fame for picturesqueness, but which struck us, in its early spring nudity, as somewhat parched and chalky-looking, without sufficient woodland to drape its angles. It makes up, however, in architectural interest for what its landscape lacks, and not many miles beyond La Châtre the otherwise featureless little town of Neuvy-Saint-Sépulcre presents one feature of unusual prominence. This is the ancient round church from which the place is named: one of those copies of the church of the Holy Sepulchre at Jerusalem with which the returning crusader dotted western Europe. Aside from their intrinsic interest, these 'sepulchre' churches have gained importance from the fact that but three or four are still extant. The most typical, that of Saint Bénigne at Dijon, has been levelled to a mere crypt, and that of Cambrige deviates from the type by reason of its octagonal dome; so that the church of Neuvy is of quite pre-eminent interest. A late Romanesque nave – itself sufficiently venerable looking to stir the imagination in its own behalf – was appended in the early thirteenth century to the circular shrine; but the latter still presents to the dull old street its unbroken cylindrical wall, built close on a thousand years ago, and surmounted, some ninety years later, by a second storey with a Romanesque exterior arcade. At this stage, however, one is left to conjecture, with the aid of expert suggestion, what manner of covering the building was meant to have. The present small dome, perched on the inner drum of the upper gallery, is an expedient of the most obvious sort; and the archæologists have inferred that the thinness of this drum may have made a more adequate form of roofing impossible.

To the idle sightseer, at any rate, the interior of the church is much more suggestive than its bare outer shell. We were happy enough to enter it toward sunset, when dusk had gathered under the heavy encircling columns, and lights twinkled yellow on the central altar which has so regrettably replaced the 'Grotto of the Sepulchre'. It was our added good fortune that a small train of the faithful, headed by a red-cassocked verger and a priest with a benignant Massillon-like head, were just making a circuit of the Stations of the Cross affixed to the walls of the aisle; and as we stood withdrawn, while the procession wound its way between shining altar and shadowy columns, some of the faces of the peasants seemed to carry us as far into the past as the strange symbolic masks on the capitals above their heads.

But what carries one farthest of all is perhaps the fact, well known to modern archæology, that the original church built by Constantine over the grotto-tomb of Christ was not a round temple at all, but a vast basilica with semi-circular apse. The Persians destroyed this building in the seventh century, and the Christians who undertook to restore it could do no more than round the circle of the apse, thus at least covering over the sacred tomb in the centre. So swift was the succession of demolition and reconstruction in that confused and clashing age, so vague and soon obliterated were the records of each previous rule, that when the crusaders came they found no memory of this earlier transformation, and carried back with them that model of the round temple which was henceforth to stand, throughout western Europe, as the venerated image of the primitive church of Jerusalem.

Too much lingering in this precious little building brought twilight on us soon after we joined the Creuse at Argenton; and when we left it again at Le Blanc lights were in the windows, and the rest of our run to Poitiers was a ghostly flight through a moon-washed landscape, with here and there a church tower looming in the dimness, or a heap of ruined walls rising mysteriously above the white bend of a river. We suffered a peculiar pang when a long-roofed pile towering overhead told us that we were passing the great Benedictine abbey of Saint Savin, with its matchless lining of frescoes; but a certain mental satiety urged us on to Poitiers.

Travellers accustomed to the marked silhouette of Italian cities – to their immediate proffer of the picturesque impression – often find the old French provincial towns lacking in physiognomy. Each Italian city, whether of the mountain or the plain, has an outline easily recognizable after individual details have faded, and it is, obviously, much easier to keep separate one's memories of Siena and Orvieto than of Bourges and Chartres. Perhaps, therefore, the few French towns with definite physiognomies seem the more definite from their infrequency; and Poitiers is foremost in this distinguished group.

Not that it offers the distinctive *galbe* of such bold hill-towns as Angoulême or Laon. Though a hill-town in fact, it somehow makes next to nothing of this advantage, and the late Mr Freeman was justified in grumbling at the lack of character in its skyline. That character reveals itself, in fact, not in any picturesqueness of distant effect – in no such far-seen crown as the towers of Laon or the domes of Périgueux – but in the homogeneous interest of the old buildings within the city: the way they carry on its packed romantic history like the consecutive pages of a richly illuminated chronicle. The illustration of that history begins with the strange little 'temple' of Saint John, a baptistery of the fourth century, and accounted the earliest Christian building in France – though this applies only to the lower storey (now virtually the crypt),

NEUVY–SAINT–SÉPULCRE: INTERIOR OF THE CHURCH

the upper having been added some three hundred years later, when baptism by aspersion had replaced the primitive plunge. Unhappily the ancient temple has suffered the lot of the too-highly treasured relic, and fenced about, restored and converted into a dry little museum, has lost all that colour and pathos of extreme age that make the charm of humbler monuments.

This charm, in addition to many others, still clings to the expressive west front of Notre Dame la Grande, the incomparable little Romanesque church holding the centre of the market-place. Built of a dark grey stone which has taken on – and been suffered to retain – a bloom of golden lichen like the trace of ancient weather-worn gilding, it breaks, at the spring of its portal-arches, into a profusion of serried, overlapping sculpture, which rises tier by tier to the splendid Christ Triumphant of the crowning gable, yet never once crowds out and smothers the structural composition, as Gothic ornament, in its most exuberant phase, was wont to do. Through all its profusion of statuary and ornamental carving, the front of Notre Dame preserves that subordination to classical composition that marks the Romanesque of southern France; but between the arches, in the great spandrils of the doorways, up to the typically Poitevin scales of the beautiful arcaded angle turrets, what richness of detail, what splendid play of fancy!

After such completeness of beauty as this little church presents – for its nave and transept tower are no less admirable than the more striking front – even such other monuments as Poitiers has to offer must suffer slightly by comparison. Saint Hilaire le Grand, that notable eleventh-century church, with its triple aisles and its nave roofed by cupolas, and the lower-lying temple of Sainte Radegonde, which dates from the Merovingian queen from whom it takes its name, have both

POITIERS: BAPTISTERY OF ST JOHN

suffered such repeated alterations that neither carries the imagination back with as direct a flight as the slightly less ancient Notre Dame; and the cathedral itself, which one somehow comes to last in an enumeration of the Poitiers churches, is a singularly charmless building. Built in the twelfth century, by Queen Eleanor of Guyenne, at the interesting moment of transition from the round to the pointed arch, and completed later by a wide-sprawling Gothic front, it gropes after and fails of its effect both without and within. Yet it has one memorable possession in its thirteenth-century choir-stalls, almost alone of that date in France – tall severe seats, their backs formed by pointed arches with delicate low-relief carvings between the spandrils. There is, in especial, one small bat, with outspread web-like wings, so exquisitely fitted into its allotted space, and with such delicacy of observation shown in the modelling of its little half-human face, that it remains in memory as having the permanence of something classical, outside of dates and styles.

Having lingered over these things, and taken in by the way an impression of the confused and rambling ducal palace, with its magnificent *grande salle* completed and adorned by Jean de Berry, we began to think remorsefully of the wonders we had missed on our run from Le Blanc to Poitiers. We could not retrace the whole distance; but at least we could return to the curious little town of Chauvigny, of which we had caught a tantalizing glimpse above a moonlit curve of the Vienne.

We found it, by day, no less suggestive, and full of unsuspected riches. Of its two large Romanesque churches, the one in the lower town, beside the river, is notable, without, for an extremely beautiful arcaded apse, and contains within a striking fresco of the fifteenth century, in which Christ is represented followed by a throng of the faithful –

POITIERS: THE CHURCH OF NOTRE-DAME-LA-GRANDE

kings, bishops, monks and clerks – who help to carry the cross. The other, and larger, church, planted on the summit of the abrupt escarpment which lifts the *haute ville* above the Vienne, has a strange bodyguard composed of no fewer than five feudal castles, huddled so close together on the narrow top of the cliff that their outer walls almost touch. The lack, in that open country, of easily fortified points doubtless drove the bishops of Poitiers (who were also barons of Chauvigny) into this strange defensive alliance with four of their noble neighbours; and one wonders how the five-sided ménage kept the peace, when local disturbances made it needful to take to the rock.

The gashed walls and ivy-draped dungeons of the rival ruins make an extraordinarily romantic setting for the curious church of Saint Pierre, staunchly seated on an extreme ledge of the cliff, and gathering under its flank the handful of town within the fortified circuit. There is nothing in architecture so suggestive of extreme age, yet of a kind of hale durability, as these thick-set Romanesque churches, with their prudent vaulting, their solid central towers, the close firm grouping of their apsidal chapels. The Renaissance brought the classic style into such permanent relationship to modern life that eleventh-century architecture seems remoter than Greece and Rome; yet its buildings have none of the perilous frailty of the later Gothic, and one associates the idea of romance and ruin rather with the pointed arch than with the round.

Saint Pierre is a singularly good example of this stout old school, which saw the last waves of barbarian invasion break at its feet, and seems likely to see the ebb and flow of so many other tides before its stubborn walls go under. It is in their sculptures, especially, that these churches reach back to a dim and fearful world of which few clues remain to us: the mysterious baleful creatures peopling their archivolts and capitals seem to have come out of some fierce vision of Cenobite temptation, when the hermits of the desert fought with the painted devils of the tombs.

The apsidal capitals of Saint Pierre are a very menagerie of such strange demons – evil beasts grinning and mocking among the stocky saints and angels who set forth, unconcerned by such hideous propinquity, the story of the birth of Christ. The animals are much more skilfully modelled than the angels, and at Chauvigny one slender monster, with greyhound flanks, sub-human face, and long curved tail ending in a grasping human hand, haunts the memory as an embodiment of subtle malevolence.

Two
POITIERS TO THE PYRENEES

THE ROAD FROM Poitiers to Angoulême carries one through a country rolling and various in line – a country with a dash of Normandy in it, but facing south instead of west.

The villages are fewer than in Normandy, and make less mark in the landscape; but the way passes through two drowsy little towns, Civray and Ruffec, each distinguished by the possession of an important church of the typical Romanesque of Poitou. That at Civray, in particular, is remarkable enough to form the object of a special pilgrimage, and to find it precisely in one's path seemed part of the general brightness of the day. Here again are the sculptured archivolt and the rich imagery of Poitiers – one strange mutilated figure of a headless horseman dominating the front from the great arcade above the doorway, as at the church of the Sainte Croix in Bordeaux; but the façade of Civray is astonishingly topped by fifteenth-century machicolations, which somehow, in spite of their later date, give it an air of greater age, of reaching back to a wild warring past.

Angoulême, set on a promontory between Charente and Anguienne, commands to the north, south and east a vast circuit of meadowy and woody undulations. The interior of the town struck one as dull, and without characteristic detail; but on the front of the twelfth-century cathedral, perched near the ledge of the cliff above the Anguienne, detail abounds as profusely as on the façade of Notre Dame at Poitiers. It is, however, so much less subordinate to the general conception that one remembers rather the garlanding of archivolts, the clustering of figures in countless niches and arcades, than the fundamental lines which should serve to bind them together; and the interior, roofed with cupolas after the manner of Saint Hilaire of Poitiers, is singularly stark and barren looking.

But when one has paid due tribute to the cathedral one is called on, from its doorway, to recognize Angoulême's other striking distinction: its splendid natural site, and the way in which art has used and made the most of it. Starting from a long leafy *cours* with private hôtels, a great avenue curves about the whole length of the walls, breaking midway into a terrace boldly hung above the valley, and ending in another leafy *place*, beneath which the slope of the hill has been skilfully transformed into a public garden. Angoulême now thrives on the manufacture of paper, and may therefore conceivably permit herself such civic adornments; but how of the many small hill-towns of France – such as Laon or Thiers, for instance – which apparently have only their past glory to subsist on, yet manage to lead up the admiring pilgrim by way of these sweeping approaches, encircling terraces and symmetrically planted esplanades? One can only salute once again the invincible French passion for form and fitness, and conclude that towns as well as nations somehow always manage to give themselves what they regard as essential, and that happy is the race to whom these things are the essentials.

On leaving Angoulême that afternoon we saw the first cypresses and the first almond blossoms. We were in the south at last; not the hot delicately pencilled Mediterranean south, which has always a hint of the East in it, but the temperate

ANGOULÊME: FAÇADE OF THE CATHEDRAL

Aquitainian *midi* cooled by the gulf of Gascony. As one nears Bordeaux the country grows less broken, the horizon-line flatter; but there is one really noble impression, when, from the bridge of Saint André de Cubzac, one looks out on the lordly sweep of the Dordogne, just before it merges its waters with the Garonne to form the great estuary of the Gironde. Soon after comes an endless dusty faubourg, then the long stone bridge over the Garonne, and the proud river-front of Bordeaux – a screen of eighteenth-century buildings stretched along the crescent-shaped quay. Bordeaux, thus approached, has indeed, as the guide-book says, *fort grand air*; and again one returns thanks to the motor, which almost always, avoiding the mean purlieus of the railway station, gives one these romantic or stately first impressions.

This river-front of Bordeaux is really little more than the architectural screen, a street or two deep, of a bustling, bright but featureless commercial town, which, from the Middle Ages to the close of the eighteenth century, seems to have crowded all its history along the curve of the Garonne. Even the early church of the Holy Cross – contemporaneous with Notre Dame la Grande of Poitiers – lifts its triple row of Romanesque arcades but a few yards from the river; and close by is Saint Michel, a stately example of late Gothic, with the unusual adjunct of a detached bell-tower, not set at an angle, in Italian fashion, but facing the church squarely from a little green enclosure across the street. But these vestiges of old Bordeaux, in spite of their intrinsic interest, are, on the whole, less characteristic, less personal, than the *mise-en-scène* of its long quay: a row of fine old hôtels with sculptured pediments and stately doorways, broken midway by the symmetrical buildings of the Exchange and the Custom House, and extending from the Arch of Triumph opposite the Pont de

THIERS: VIEW OF THE TOWN FROM THE PONT DE SEYCHALLES

Bordeaux to the great Place des Quinconces, with its rostral columns and balustraded terrace above the river.

To the modern traveller there is food for thought in the fact that Bordeaux owes this great decorative composition – in which should be included the theatre unfolding its majestic peristyle at the head of the Place de la Comédie – to the magnificent taste and free expenditure of the Intendant Tourny, who ruled the province of Guyenne in the eighteenth century. Except at such high moments of æsthetic sensibility as produced the monuments of Greece and republican Italy all large schemes of civic adornment have been due to the initiative of one man, and executed without much regard to the rights of the taxpayer; and should the citizen of a modern republic too rashly congratulate himself on exemption from the pillage productive of such results, he might with equal reason remark that the tribute lawfully extracted from him sometimes seems to produce no results whatever.

On leaving Bordeaux we deserted the *route nationale* along the flat west bank of the Garonne, and recrossing the Pont de Bordeaux ran south through the white-wine region between Garonne and Dordogne – that charming strip of country which, because of the brackishness of the river tides, goes by the unexpected name of Entre-deux-Mers. For several miles we skirted a line of white houses, half villa, half château, set in well-kept gardens; then came vineyards, as exquisitely kept, and packed into every cranny of the rocky *coteaux*, save where here and there a little town broke the view of the river – chief among them Langoiron, with its fine fortress-ruin, and Cadillac enclosed in stout quadrangular walls.

The latter place has the interest of being one of those

BORDEAUX: CHURCH OF THE HOLY CROSS

symmetrically designed towns which, toward the close of the Middle Ages, were founded throughout south-western France to draw 'back to the land' a population depleted and demoralized by long years of warfare and barbarian invasion. These curious made-to-order towns – *bastides* or *villes neuves* – were usually laid out on a rectilinear plan, with a town hall forming the centre of an arcaded market-place, to which four streets led from gateways in the four walls. Among the most characteristic examples are Aigues Mortes, which Saint Louis called into existence to provide himself with a Mediterranean port, and Cordes, near Gaillac, founded a little later by Count Raymond of Toulouse, and somewhat ambitiously named by him after the city of Cordova.

At Cadillac the specific physiognomy of the mediæval *bastide* is overshadowed by the lofty proportions and high-pitched roof of the château which a sixteenth-century Duke of Epernon planted in an angle of the walls. The adjoining parish church – itself of no mean dimensions – was once but the private chapel of these same dukes, who have left such a large architectural impress on their small shabby town; and one grieves to learn that the chief monument of their rule has fallen to base uses, and been stripped of the fine interior decorations which its majestic roof once sheltered.

South-west of Cadillac the road passes through a vast stretch of pine forest with a dry aromatic undergrowth – an outskirt of the great *landes* that reach inward from the gulf of Gascony. On and on runs the white shadow-barred highway, between ranges of red boles and sun-flecked heathy clearings – and when, after long hours, one emerges from the unwonted mystery and solitude of this piny desert into the usual busy agricultural France, the land is breaking southward into hilly waves, and beyond the hills are the Pyrenees.

Yet one's first real sight of them – so masked are they by lesser ranges – is got next day from the terrace at Pau, that astonishing balcony hung above the great amphitheatre of south-western France. Seen thus, with the prosaic English-provincial-looking town at one's back, and the park-like green *coteaux* intervening beyond the Gave, the austere white peaks, seemingly afloat in heaven (for their base is almost always lost in mist), have a disconcerting look of irrelevance, of dispro-portion, of being subjected to a kind of indignity of inspection, like caged carnivora in a zoo.

And Pau, on farther acquaintance, utterly refuses to be brought into any sort of credible relation with its great southern horizon; conducts itself, architecturally and socially, like a comfortable little spa in a plain, and rises only by a great deal of hoisting on the part of the imaginative sight-seer to the height of its own dapper brick castle, which it has domesticated into an empty desultory museum, and tethered down with a necklet of turf and flowers.

But Pau's real purpose is to serve as the hub of a great wheel, of which the spokes, made of smooth white roads, radiate away into every fold and cleft of the country. As a centre for excursions there is no place like it in France, because there is nothing in France that quite matches the sweetness and diversity of the long Pyrenean border. Nowhere else are the pastoral and sylvan so happily mated, nowhere the villages so compact of thrift and romance, the foreground so sweet, the distances so sublime and shining.

Whichever way one turns – down the winding southern valleys toward Lourdes and Argelès, or to Oloron and the Eaux Chaudes; westward, over low hills, to the old town of

Orthez and the Salies de Béarn; or east, again, to the plain of Tarbes in its great ring of snow-peaks – always there is the same fullness of impressions, always the same brightness and the same nobility.

For a culminating instance of these impressions one might choose, on a spring afternoon, the run to Lourdes by the valley of the Gave and Bétharram.

First rich meadows, hedgerows, village streets; then fields again and hills; then the brown rush of the Gave between wooded banks; and, where the river threads the arch of an ivied bridge, the turreted monastery walls and pilgrimage church of Bétharram – a deserted seventeenth-century Lourdes, giving one a hint of what the modern sanctuary might have been had the millions spent on it been drawn from the faithful when piety still walked with art.

Bétharram, since its devotees have forsaken it, is a quite negligible 'sight', relegated to small type even in the copious Joanne; yet in view of what is coming it is worth while to pause before its half-Spanish, half-Venetian church front, and to obey the suave yet noble gesture with which the Virgin above the doorway calls her pilgrims in.

She has only a low brown church to show, with heavy stucco angels spreading their gilded wings down a perspective of incense-fogged baroque; but the image of it will come back when presently, standing under the big dome of the Lourdes 'Basilica', one gives thanks that modern piety chose to build its own shrine instead of laying hands on an old one.

There are two Lourdes, the 'grey' and the 'white'. The former, undescribed and unvisited, is simply one of the most picturesque and feudal-looking hill villages in Europe. Planted on a steep rock at the mouth of the valley, the mountains pressing it close to the west and south, it opposes its unbroken walls and stern old keep to the other, the 'white' town sprawling on the river bank – the town of the Basilica, the Rosary, the Grotto: a congeries of pietistic hotels, *pensions*, pedlars' booths and panoramas, where the Grand Hôtel du Casino or du Palais adjoins the Pension de la Première Apparition, and the blue-sashed Vierge de Lourdes on the threshold calls attention to the electric light and *déjeuner par petites tables* within.

Out of this vast sea of vulgarism – the more aggressive and intolerable because its last waves break against one of the loveliest landscapes of this lovely country – rises what the uninstructed tourist might be pardoned for regarding as the casino of an eminently successful watering-place – as the Grotto beneath, with its drinking-fountains, baths, bottling-taps and *boutiques*, might stand for the 'Source' or 'Brunnen' where the hypochondriac pays toll to Hygieia before seeking relaxation in the gilded halls above. For the shrine of Berna-dette has long since been overlaid by the machinery of a vast 'business enterprise', a scheme of life in which every heart-beat is itemized, tariffed and exploited, so that even the invocations encrusting by thousands the Basilica walls seem to record so many cases of definite 'give and take', so many bargains struck with heaven – *en souvenir de mon vœu, reconnais-sance pour une guérison, souvenir d'une prière exaucée*, and so on – and as one turns away from this monument of a thriving industry one may be pardoned for remembering the plane-tree by the Ilissus and another invocation: 'Ye gods, give me beauty in the inward soul; and may the inner and the outer man be one.'

But beyond Lourdes is Argelès, and at the first turn of the road one is again in the fresh Pyrenean country, among budding crops, sleek fawn-coloured cattle, and the grave

BÉTHARRAM: THE BRIDGE

handsome peasantry who make one feel that the devotional *ville d'eaux* one has just left is a mushroom growth quite unrelated to the life of industry to which these agricultural landscapes testify.

There is always an added interest – architectural and racial – about the border regions where the idiosyncrasies of one people 'run', as it were, into those adjoining; and a key to the character of each is given by noting precisely what traits have survived in transplantation. The Pyreneans have a certain Spanish seriousness, but so tempered by Gallic good humour that their address recalls the perfectly mingled courtesy and self-respect of the Tuscan peasant. One feels in it, at any rate, the result of an old civilization blent with independence and simplicity of living; and these bold handsome men, straight of feature and limb, seem the natural product of their rich hill country, so disciplined by industry, yet so romantically free.

Argelès is a charming old hill-town, which has kept itself quite aloof from the new watering-place of Gazost in the plain; but the real object of the excursion lies higher up the valley, in a chestnut forest on the slope of the mountains. Here the tiny village of Saint Savin swarms bee-like about its great Romanesque church – a naked massive structure, like the skeleton of some prehistoric animal half emerging from the rock. Old as it is, it is rooted in remains of greater antiquity – the fallen walls of an abbey of Charlemagne's building, itself raised, the legend runs, on the site of a Roman villa which once served as the hermitage of Saint Savin, son of a Count of Barcelona.

It has been the fate of too many venerable architectural relics to sacrifice their bloom of *vetusté* to the scrupulous care which makes them look like conscious cosseted old ladies, of whom their admiring relatives say: 'Should you ever suspect

ARGELÉS–GAZOST: THE OLD BRIDGE

her age?' – and only in such remote monuments as that of Saint Savin does one get the sense of undisguised antiquity, of a long stolid existence exposed to every elemental influence. The result is an impression of rugged, taciturn strength, and of mysterious memories striking back, as in the holy-water basin of the transept, and the uncouth capitals of the chapter house, to those dark days when Christian civilization hung in the balance, and the horn of Roland sounded down the pass.

But a mediæval church is always more or less in the order of nature: there is something more incongruous about a mediæval watering-place. Yet the Pyrenees abound in them; and at Cauterets, farther up the same valley, the monks of this very monastery of Saint Savin maintained, in the tenth century, 'habitations to facilitate the use of the baths'. Of the original Cauterets, however, little remains, and to get an impression of an old *ville d'eaux* one must turn westward from Pau, and strike across the hills, by ways of exceeding beauty, to the Salies de Béarn. The frequentation of these saline springs dates back as far as the monkish charter of Cauterets; and the old town of the Salies, with its incredibly picturesque half-timbered houses, its black balconies and gables above the river, looks much as it must have when, in 1587, a charter was drawn up for the regular 'exploitation' of the baths.

Pushing still farther westward one meets the highway to Bayonne and Biarritz, and may thence pass south by Saint Jean de Luz and Hendaye to the Spanish border. But the spokes of the wheel radiate in so many different directions and lead to scenes so extraordinarily varied – from the savage gorge of the Eaux-Chaudes to the smiling vale of Saint Jean Pied-de-Port, from the romantic pass of the Pied de Roland to Fontarrabia perched like a painted Spanish Virgin on its rock above the gulf of Gascony – that to do them any sort of justice the

SALIES DE BÉARN: VIEW OF OLD TOWN

comet-flight of the motor would have to be bound down to an orbit between Bidassoa and Garonne.

Familiarity cannot blunt the wonder of the climb from Pau to the crest of the hills above Tarbes. Southward the Pyrenees unfold themselves in a long line of snows, and ahead every turn of the road gives a fresh glimpse of wood and valley, of thriving villages and farms, till the last jut of the ridge shows Tarbes far off in the plain, with the dim folds of the Cévennes clouding the eastern distance.

All along the north-eastern skirt of the Pyrenees runs the same bright and opulent country; and at the old market town of Montrejeau, where the Garonne cuts its way down the vale of Luchon, there is just such a fortunate grouping of hill and river, and distant high-perched ruin, as our grandparents admired in landscapes of the romantic school. It was our good luck to enter Montrejeau on Easter Monday, while the market was going on, and the narrow streets were packed with mild cream-coloured cattle and their lively blue-smocked drivers. Great merriment and general good humour marked our passage through the town to the big inn with its open galleries and old-fashioned courtyard; and here, the dining-room being as packed as the streets, our table was laid in a sunny old walled garden full of spring flowers and clipped yews.

It seemed impossible that any incident of the afternoon should be quite at the height of this gay repast, consumed in fragrance and sunshine; but we began to think differently when, an hour or two later, we took the first curve of the long climb to Saint Bertrand de Comminges. This atom of a town, hugging a steep wedge of rock at the mouth of the vale of Luchon, was once – and for many centuries – a diocesan seat; and who, by all the spirits of incongruousness, should one of its last bishops be, but the uncle of that acute and lively Madame de Boigne whose memoirs have recently shed such light on the last days of the Old Régime?

By no effort of imagination can one project into the single perpendicular street of Saint Bertrand, topped by its rugged Gothic cathedral, the gallant figure of Monseigneur Dillon, one of those philosophical prelates whom one instinctively places against the *lambris dorés* of an episcopal palace hung with Boucher tapestries. But in truth the little town has too old and strange a history to be conscious of so fugitive an incident of its past. For its foundations were laid by the mountain tribes who harassed Pompey's legions and were driven back by him into the valley of the Garonne; and in due time a great temple rose on what is now the rock of the cathedral. Walls and ramparts presently enclosed it, and the passage of the Vandals having swept the dwellers of the plain back into this impregnable circuit, Comminges became an episcopal city when the Catholic Church was organized in Gaul. Thereafter it underwent all the vicissitudes of barbarian invasion, falling at last into such decay that for five hundred years it is said to have been without inhabitants. Yet the episcopal line was maintained without more than one long break, and in the eleventh century the diocese woke to life at the call of its saintly Bishop, Bertrand de l'Isle Jourdain. Saint Bertrand began the cathedral and built about it the mediæval town which bears his name: and two hundred years later another Bertrand de Comminges, raised to the papacy as Clement V, but still mindful of the welfare of his former diocese, completed the Romanesque pile by the addition of a vast Gothic nave and choir.

It is the church of Clement V that still crowns the rock of

Comminges, contrasting by its monumental proportions with the handful of houses enclosed in the walls at its base. The inhabitants of Comminges number at present but some five hundred, and the town subsists, the guide-books tell one, only on its religious festivals, the fame of its monuments, and the fidelity of a few 'old families' who are kept there *par le prestige des souvenirs*.

One wonders, climbing the steep street, which of its decrepit houses are inhabited by these interesting devotees of the past. No life is visible save that contributed by a few bleary old women squatted under mouldering arches, and a fire-fly dance of children about the stony square before the church; and the church itself seems withdrawn immeasurably far into the past, sunk back upon dim ancient memories of Gaul and Visigoth.

One gets an even intenser sense of these distances from the little cloister wedged against the church-flank and overhanging the radiant valley of the Garonne – a queer cramped *enceinte*, with squat arches supported by monster-girdled capitals, and in one case by a strange group of battered figures, supposedly the four Evangelists, one of whom – the Saint John – is notable in Romanesque archæology for bearing in his arms the limp lamb which is his attribute.

The effect of antiquity is enhanced, as at Saint Savin, by the beneficent neglect which has allowed the exterior of the building to take on all the scars and hues of age; so that one comes with a start of surprise on the rich and carefully tended interior, where a brilliant bloom of Renaissance decoration has overlaid the stout Gothic framework.

This airy curtain, masking choir, rood-screen and organ-loft in a lace-work of delicate yet hardy wood-carving, has kept, in the dry Pyrenean air, all its sharpness of detail,

ST BERTRAND–DE–COMMINGES: PIER OF THE FOUR
EVANGELISTS IN THE CLOISTER

acquiring only a lustre of surface that gives it almost the texture of old bronze. It is wonderfully free and fanciful, yet tempered by the southern sense of form; subdued to the main lines of the composition, but breaking into the liveliest ripples of leaf and flower, of bird and sprite and angel, till its audacities culminate in the scaly undulations of the mermaids on the terminal seats of the choir – creatures of bale and beauty, who seem to have brought from across the Alps their pagan eyes and sidelong Lombard smile.

The finger-tailed monster of Chauvigny, the plaintively real bat of the choir-stall at Poitiers, and these siren evocations of a classic past group themselves curiously in the mind as embodiments of successive phases of human fancy, imaginative interpretations of life.

Three

THE PYRENEES TO PROVENCE

A s one turns north-eastward from the Pyrenees the bright abundant landscape passes gradually into a flattish grey-and-drab country that has ceased to be Aquitaine and is yet not Provence.

A dull region at best, this department of Haute Garonne grows positively forbidding when the mistral rakes it, whitening the vineyards and mulberry orchards, and bowing the shabby cypresses against a confused grey sky; nor is the landscape redeemed by the sprawling silhouette of Toulouse – a dingy wind-ridden city, stretched wide on the flat banks of the Garonne, and hiding its two precious buildings in a network of mean brick streets.

One might venture the general axiom that France has never wholly understood the use of brick, and that where stone construction ceases architectural beauty ceases with it. Saint Sernin, the great church of Toulouse, is noble enough in line, and full of interest as marking the culmination of French Romanesque; but compared with the brick churches of northern Italy it seems struck with aridity, parched and bleached as a skeleton in a desert. The Capitoul, with its frivolous eighteenth-century front, has indeed more warmth and relief than any other building in Toulouse; but meanly surrounded by shabby brick houses, it seems to await in vain the development of ramps and terraces that should lead up to its long bright façade.

As the motor enters the hill-country to the north-east of Toulouse the land breaks away pleasantly toward the long blue line of the Cévennes; and presently a deep cleft fringed with green reveals the nearness of the Tarn – that strange river gnawing its way through cheesy perpendicular banks.

Along these banks fantastic brick towns are precariously piled: L'Isle-sur-Tarn, with an octagonal brick belfry, and Rabastens, raised on a series of bold arcaded terraces, which may be viewed to advantage from a suspension bridge high above the river. Aside from its exceptionally picturesque site, Rabastens is notable for a curious brick church with fortified tower and much-restored fourteenth-century frescoes clothing its interior like a dim richly woven tissue. But beyond Rabastens lies Albi, and after a midday halt at Gaillac, most desolate and dusty of towns, we pressed on again through the parched country.

Albi stood out at length upon the sky – a glaring mass of houses stacked high above the deep cleft of the Tarn. The surrounding landscape was all dust and dazzle; the brick streets were funnels for the swooping wind; and high up, against the blinding blue, rose the flanks of the brick cathedral, like those of some hairless pink monster that had just crawled up from the river to bask on the cliff. This first impression of animal monstrosity – of an unwieldy antediluvian mass of flesh – is not dispelled by a nearer approach. From whatever angle one views the astounding building its uncouth shape and flesh-like tint produce the effect of a living organism – high-backed, swollen-thighed, wallowing – a giant Tarasque or other anomalous offspring of the Bestiary; and if one rejects the animal analogy as too grotesque, to what else may one conceivably compare it?

Among the fortified churches of south-western France this

ALBI: GENERAL VIEW OF THE CATHEDRAL

strange monument is the strangest as it is the most vast, and none of the accepted architectural categories seems to fit its huge vaulted hall buttressed with tall organ-pipe turrets, and terminating to the west in a massive dungeon-like tower flanked by pepper-pot pinnacles.

The interior of the great secular-looking *salle* is covered by an unbroken expanse of mural painting, and encrusted, over-grown almost, from the choir and ambulatory to the arches of the lateral chapels with a prodigious efflorescence of late Gothic wood-carving and sculpture, half Spanish in its dusky grey-brown magnificence. But even this excess of ecclesiastical ornament does not avail to Christianize the church – there is a pagan, a Saracenic quality about it that seems to overflow from its pinnacled flushed exterior.

To reach Carcassonne from Albi one must cross the central mass of the Cévennes. The way leads first, by hill and dale, through a wooded northern-looking landscape, to the town of Castres, distinguished by a charming *hôtel de ville* with a box-planted garden said to have been laid out by Le Nôtre; and soon after Castres the 'wild-ridged steeps' break away in widening undulations as the road throws its loops about the sides of the Montagne Noire – black hollows deepening dizzily below, and long grey vistas unfolding between the crowded peaks. Unhappily a *bourrasque* enveloped us before we reached the top of the pass, so that we lost all the beauty of the long southern descent to Carcassonne, and were aware of it only as a distant tangle of lights in the plain, toward which we groped painfully through wind and rain.

The rain persisted the next day; but perhaps it is a not undesirable accompaniment to a first view of Carcassonne, since it eliminates that tout-and-tourist element which has so possessed itself of the ancient *cité*, restoring to it, under a

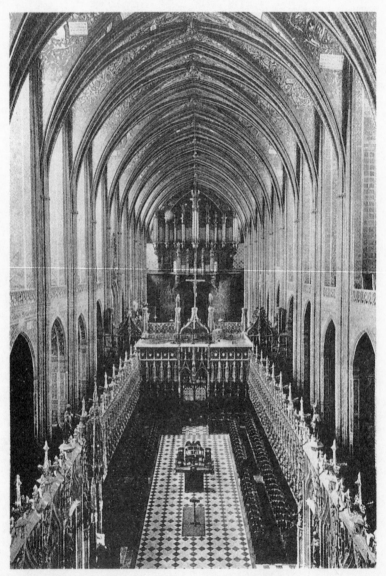

ALBI: INTERIOR OF THE CATHEDRAL

grey blurred light, something of its narrow huddled mediæval life.

He who has gone there with wrath in his heart against Viollet-le-Duc may even, under these mitigating conditions, go so far as to think that the universal restorer has for once been justified by his results – that, granting in advance the possibility of innumerable errors of detail, his brilliant hypothesis still produces a total impression of reality. Perhaps, too, all the floating tags of literary mediævalism – the irresistible 'connotations' of keep and rampart and portcullis – help out the illusion, animate the serried little burgh, and people it with such figures as Dante walked among when Bellincion Berti went girt with leather. At any rate, the impression is there – for those who have the hardihood to take it – there all the more palpably on a day of such unbroken rain, when even the official custodians hug their stove, and a beneficent mist hides the stacks of postcards and souvenirs waylaying the traveller from every window.

The weather, however, so beneficent at Carcassonne, proved an obstacle to the seeing of Narbonne and Béziers, and drove us relentlessly before it to Nîmes, where it gave us, the next morning, one of those brilliant southern days that are born of the southern deluges. Here was Provence at last – dry, clear-edged, classic – with a sky like blue marble, low red hills tufted by olives, stony hollows with thin threads of stream, and a sun that picked out in gold the pure curves of the Maison Carrée.

Among the Greek towns of the Mediterranean there is none as Greek – or, to speak more precisely, as Græco-Roman – as Nîmes. No other city of old Gaul seems to have put itself so completely in harmony with its rich nucleus of 'remains' eliminating or omitting the monuments of other periods, and

NÎMES: THE BATHS OF DIANA – PUBLIC GARDENS

content to group its later growth subserviently about the temple and the amphitheatre. It was very well for Arles to make its Romanesque venture, for Rheims to crown itself with a glory of Gothic; but with the tranquil lines of the Maison Carrée and the Nymphæum, the rhythmic spring of the arena arches, to act as centralizing influences – above all with the overwhelming grandeur of the Pont du Gard as a background – how could Nîmes, so far more deeply pledged to the past, do otherwise than constitute herself the guardian of great memories? The Pont du Gard alone would be enough to relegate any town to a state of ancillary subjection. Its nearness is as subduing as that of a great mountain, and next to the Mont Ventoux it is the sublimest object in Provence. The solitude of its site, and the austere lines of the surrounding landscape, make it appear as much on the outer edge of civilization as when it was first planted there; and its long defile of arches seems to be forever pushing on into the wilderness with the tremendous tread of the Roman legions.

By one of the charming oppositions of French travel, one may return from this classic pilgrimage through the mediæval town of Uzès; and, as if such contrasts were not fruitful enough, may pause on the way to smile at the fantastic château d'Angivilliers – a half-ruined eighteenth-century 'Folly' with an anachronistic medley of kiosks, arcades, pagodas, a chapel like a Roman temple, and a ruined box-garden haunted by peacocks.

Uzès itself, a steep town clustered about the ducal keep of the Crussols, has a stately terrace above the valley, and some fine eighteenth-century houses, in shabby streets insufficiently swept; but its chief feature is of course the castle which, planted protectingly in the centre of the town, thrusts up

CARCASSONNE: THE PORTE DE L'AUDE

its central dungeon over a fine feudal jumble of subsidiary masonry.

From Nîmes to the Mediterranean the impressions are packed too thick. First the Rhône, with the castles of Tarascon and Beaucaire taunting each other across its yellow flood, Beaucaire from a steep cliff, Tarascon from the very brink of the river; then, after a short flight through olive orchards and vineyards, the pretty leafy town of Saint Rémy on the skirts of the Alpilles; and a mile to the south of Saint Rémy, on a chalky ledge of the low mountain-chain, the two surviving monuments of the Roman city of Glanum. They are set side by side, the tomb and the triumphal arch, in a circular grassy space enclosed with olive orchards and backed by delicate fretted peaks: not another vestige of Roman construction left to connect them with the past. Was it, one wonders, their singular beauty that saved them, that held even the Visigoths' hands when they wiped out every other trace of the populous city of stone-quarriers, with its aqueducts, walls and temples? Certainly, seeing the two buildings thus isolated under the radiant lonely sky, one is tempted to exclaim that they might well have checked even barbarian violence, and that never again did the stout Roman trunk throw out two such flowers of grace and lightness. It is as though, from that packed Provençal soil, some dust of Greece had passed into the Latin stem, clearing a little its thick sap; yet it is just because the monuments remain so sturdily Roman that the grace and the lightness count so much.

This Alpilles country between Rhône and Durance is itself the most Grecian thing west of Greece: Provence of Provence in every line of its bare sharp-cut heights, tufted with a spare classic growth of olive, cistus and myrtle, it explains why the Greek colonist found himself at home on these ultimate

SAINT-RÉMY: THE MAUSOLEUM

shores, and why the Roman conqueror bowed here to Attic influences.

Pushing south-east from Saint Rémy, one comes, through a broadening landscape, to the old town of Salon, where Nostradamus is buried, and thence, by a winding road among the hills, to the wide valley where Aix-en-Provence lies encircled in mountains.

For a town so nobly seated it seems, at first approach, a little commonplace and insignificant; the eye, lighting on it from the heights, seeks a sky-line like that of Clermont or Périgueux. Aix, in this respect, remains inadequate; yet presents itself to closer inspection as a charming faded old place, tinged with legal and academic memories, with a fine double row of balconied and sculptured hôtels along its leafy *cours*, and a number of scattered treasures in the folds of its crooked streets.

Among these treasures the two foremost – the picture of the *Buisson Ardent* in the cathedral, and the Gobelin tapestries in the adjoining Archbishop's palace – belong to such widely sundered schools that they might almost be said to represent the extreme points within which French art has vibrated. It is therefore the more interesting to note that both are intrinsically and pre-eminently decorative in quality – devotional triptych and frivolous tapestry obeying the same law of rigorously balanced lines and colours. The great picture of the Burning Bush is, with the exception of the Virgin of Moulins, perhaps the finest flower of that early French school of painting which was so little known or considered that, until the recent Paris exhibition of 'Primitives', many of its masterpieces were complacently attributed to Italian painters. Hanging midway down the nave, where a golden light strikes it when the sacristan flings open the splendid carved doors of the west front, the triptych of Nicholas Froment unfolds itself like a great three-petalled flower, each leaf burning with a rich limpidity of colour that overflows from the Rosa Mystica of the central panel to the pale prayerful faces of the royal donators in the wings.

The cathedral has its tapestries also – a series from the Brussels looms, attributed to Quentin Matsys, and covering the choir with intricately composed scenes from the life of Christ, in which the melancholy grey-green of autumn leaves is mingled with deep jewel-like pools of colour. But these are accidental importations from another world, whereas the famous Don Quixote series in the Archbishop's palace represents the culminating moment of French decorative art.

They strike one perhaps, first of all – these rosy *chatoyantes* compositions, where ladies in loosened bodices gracefully prepare to be 'surprised' – as an instructive commentary on ecclesiastical manners toward the close of the eighteenth century; then one passes on to abstract enjoyment of their colour-scheme and balance of line, to a delighted perception of the way in which they are kept from being (as tapestries later became) mere imitations of painting, and remain imprisoned – yet so free! – in that fanciful textile world which has its own flora and fauna, its own laws of colour and perspective, and its own more-than-Shakespearian anachronisms in costume and architecture.

From Aix to the Mediterranean the south-eastern highway passes through a land of ever-increasing loveliness. East of Aix the bare-peaked mountain of Sainte Victoire dominates the fertile valley for long miles. Then the hermit-haunted range of the Sainte Baume unfolds its wooded flanks to the south, the highway skirting them as it gradually mounts to the plateau where the town of Saint Maximin clusters about its unfinished

Dominican church – a remarkable example of northern Gothic strayed into the classic confines of Provence.

Saint Maximin owes its existence – or that part of it contingent on possessing so important a church – to the ownership of the bones of Saint Mary Magdalen, whose supposed relics were formerly venerated in the great Burgundian church of Vézelay, but in the thirteenth century were officially identified among the treasures of the Provençal town. As the penitent saint is supposed to have spent her last years in a grotto on the heights of the Sainte Baume, it seems more fitting that she should now rest at its foot than on the far-off rock of the Morvan; and one is glad that the belief was early enough established to produce the picturesque anomaly of this fine fragment of northern art planted against the classic slopes of the Maritime Alps.

The great Gothic church was never finished, without or within; but in the seventeenth century a renewal of devotion to Saint Mary Magdalen caused the interior of the choir to be clothed with a magnificent *revêtement* of wood-carving in the shape of ninety-two choir-stalls, recounting in their sculptured medallions the history of the Dominican order, and leading up to a sumptuous Berniniesque high altar, all jasper, porphyry and shooting rays of gold.

Saint Maximin, though lying so remotely among bare fields and barer mountains, still shows, outside its church, some interesting traces of former activity and importance. A stout old Dominican monastery extends its long row of ogival windows near the church, and here and there a vigorous bit of ancient masonry juts from the streets – notably in the sprawling arcades of the Jewish quarter, and where certain fragments of wall attest that the mountain village was once a strongly defended mediæval town.

ST MAXIMIN: CHOIR STALLS IN THE CHURCH

Beyond Saint Maximin the *route nationale* bears away between the mountains to Nice; but at Brignoles – a city of old renown, the winter residence of the Counts of Provence – one may turn southward, by Roquebrussanne and the Chartreuse of Montrieux (where Petrarch's brother was abbot), to the radiant valley of the Gapeau, where the stream-side is already white with cherry blossoms, and so at length come out, at Hyères, on the full glory of the Mediterranean spring.

One's first feeling is that nothing else matches it – that no work of man, no accumulated appeal of history, can contend a moment against this joy of the eye so prodigally poured out. The stretch of coast from Toulon to Saint Tropez, so much less familiar to northern eyes than the more eastern portion of the Riviera, has a peculiar nobility, a Virgilian breadth of composition, in marked contrast to the red-rocked precipitous landscape beyond. Looking out on it from the pine-woods of Costebelle, above Hyères, one is beset by classic allusions, analogies of the golden age – so divinely does the green plain open to the sea, between mountain lines of such Attic purity.

After packed weeks of historic and archæological sensation this surrender to the spell of the landscape tempts one to indefinite idling. It is the season when, through the winter verdure of the Riviera, spring breaks with a hundred tender tints – pale green of crops, white snow of fruit blossoms, and fire of scarlet tulips under the grey smoke of olive-groves. From heights among the cork trees the little towns huddled about their feudal keeps blink across the pine forests at the dazzling blue-and-purple indentations of the coast. And between the heights mild valleys widen down – valleys with fields of roses, acres of budding vine, meadows sown with narcissus, and cold streams rushing from the chestnut forests below the bald grey peaks. Among the peaks are lonely hermitages, ruined remains of old monastic settlements, Carthusian and Benedictine; but no great names are attached to these fallen shrines, and the little towns below have no connection with the main lines of history. It is all a tranquil backwater, thick with local tradition, little floating fragments of association and legend; but art and history seem to have held back from it, as from some charmed Elysian region, too calm, too complete, to be rudely touched to great issues.

It was the mistral that drove us from this den, poisoning it with dust and glare, and causing us to take refuge north of the seaboard Alps. There, in a blander air and on a radiant morning, we left Aix behind, and followed the Durance to Avignon. Approaching the papal city from the east, one may get a memorable impression by following the outer circuit of its walls to the Porte de l'Ouille, which opens on the Place Crillon just below the great rock of the palace. Seen thus from without, Avignon is like a toy model of a mediæval city; and this impression of artificial completeness is renewed when, from the rock-perched terrace below the palace, one looks out on the Rhône valley and its enclosing amphitheatre of mountains. In the light Provençal air, which gives a finely pencilled precision to the remotest objects, the landscape has an extraordinarily topographical character, an effect of presenting with a pre-Raphaelite insistence on detail its sharp-edged ruins, its turreted bridge, its little walled towns on definite points of rock. The river winding through the foreground holds its yellow curve between thin fringes of poplar and sharp calcareous cliffs; and even the remoter hills have the clear

silhouette of the blue peaks in mediæval miniatures, the
shoulder of the Mont Ventoux rising above them to the north
with the firmness of an antique marble.

This southern keenness of edge gives even to the Gothicism
of the piled-up church and palace an exotic, transalpine
quality, and makes the long papal ownership of Avignon –
lasting, it is well to remember, till the general upheaval of
1790 – a visible and intelligible fact. Though the Popes of
Avignon were Frenchmen, Avignon is unmistakably, almost
inexplicably, Italian: its Gothic vaguely suggests that of the
Ponte Sant' Angelo, of the fortified arches and tombs of
mediæval Rome, and reconciles itself as easily to the florid
façade of the seventeenth-century Papal Mint in the square
below as to the delicate classic detail of the west door of the
church.

Rome – but Imperial not Papal Rome – was still in the air
as we left Avignon and followed the Rhône valley northward
to Orange. All this part of France is thick with history, and in
the ancient principality of Orange the layers are piled so deep
that one wonders to see so few traces of successive dominations
in the outward aspect of its capital. Only the Rome of the
Emperors has left a mark on the town which lived with so
vigorous and personal life from the days when it was a Gaulish
city and a trading station of Massaliote Greeks, and which,
when it grew too small for its adventurous brood, sent rulers
to both shores of the North Sea; and the fact that the theatre
and the arch survive, while the Orange of Carlovingian
bishops and mediæval princes has been quite wiped out, and
even Maurice of Nassau's great seventeenth-century fortress
razed to the ground – this permanence of the imperial
monuments, rising unshaken through the blown dust of nearly
a thousand years, gives a tangible image of the way in which

TOULON: THE HOUSE OF PUGET

the Roman spirit has persisted through the fluctuations of history.

To learn that these very monuments have been turned to base uses by barbarous prince-bishops – the arch converted into a fortified Château de l'Arc, the theatre into an outwork of the main fortress – adds impressiveness to their mutilated splendour, awing one with the image of a whole reconstructed from such fragments.

Among these, the theatre, now quite stripped of ornament, produces its effect only by means of its size, and of the beautiful sweep of its converging lines; but the great golden-brown arch – standing alone in a wide grassy square – keeps on three sides a Corinthian mask of cornice and column, and a rich embossing of fruit and flower-garlands, of sirens, trophies and battle-scenes. All this decoration is typically Roman – vigorously carved and somewhat indiscriminately applied. One looks in vain for the sensitive ornament of the arch of Saint Rémy, in which Mérimée's keen eye saw a germ of the coming Gothic: the sculpture of Orange follows the conventional lines of its day, without showing a hint of new forms. But that very absence of imaginative suggestion makes it Roman and imperial to the core.

Ahead of us, all the way from Avignon to Orange, the Mont Ventoux lifted into the pure light its denuded flanks and wrinkled silvery-lilac summit. But at Orange we turned about its base, and bore away north-eastward through a broken country rimmed with hills, passing by Tulette, the seat of a Cluniac foundation – of which the great Rovere, Julius II, was Prince and Prior – and by Valréas, which under the Popes of Avignon became the capital of the Haut Comtat, the French papal dominion in France.

Like too many old towns in this part of France, Valréas,

ORANGE: THE ARCH OF MARIUS

once a strongly fortified place, has suffered its castle to fall in ruins, and swept away its towers and ramparts to make room for boulevards, as though eager to efface all traces of its long crowded past. But one such trace – nearer at hand and of more intimate connotations – remains in the Hôtel de Simiane, now the *hôtel de ville*, but formerly the house of that Marquis de Simiane who married Pauline de Grignan, the grand-daughter of Madame de Sévigné.

This is the first reminder that we are in the Grignan country, and that a turn of the road will presently bring us in full view of that high-perched castle where the great lieutenant-governor of Provence, Madame de Sévigné's son-in-law, dispensed an almost royal hospitality and ruled with more than royal arrogance.

The Comte de Grignan was counted a proud man, and there was much to foster pride in the site and aspect of his ancestral castle – *ce château royal de Grignan*. If Italy, and papal Italy, has been in one's mind at every turn of the way from Avignon to Tulette, it seems actually to rise before one as the great ruin, springing suddenly from its cliff in the plain, evokes a not too audacious comparison with the rock of Caprarola. In France, at least, there is perhaps nothing as suggestive of the fortified pleasure-houses of Italy as this gallant castle on the summit of its rock, with the town clustering below, and the vast terrace before it actually forming the roof of its church. And the view from the terrace has the same illimitable sun-washed spaces, flowing on every side into noble mountain-forms, from the Mont Ventoux in the south to the range of the Ardèche in the west.

The ancient line of Adhémar, created Counts of Grignan by Henri II, had long been established on their rocky pedestal when they built themselves, in the sixteenth century, the

GRIGNAN: THE GATE OF THE CASTLE

magnificent Renaissance façade of which only the angle
towers now subsist. Later still they added the great gallery
lined with full-length portraits of the Adhémar, and under
Louis XIV Mansart built the so-called *Façade des Prélats*, which
judging from its remains, did not yield in stateliness to any of
the earlier portions of the castle. From this side a fine flight of
double steps still descends to a garden set with statues and
fountains; and beyond it lies the vast stone terrace which forms
the roof of the collegial church, and is continued by a *chemin
de ronde* crowning the lofty ramparts on the summit of the
rock.

This princely edifice remained in unaltered splendour for
sixty years after the house of Adhémar, in the person of
Madame de Sévigné's grandson, had died out, ruined and
diminished, in 1732. But when the Revolution broke, old
memories of the Comte de Grignan's dealings with his people
– of unpaid debts, extorted loans, obscure lives devoured by
the greedy splendour on the rock – all these recollections, of
which one may read the record in various family memoirs, no
doubt increased the fury of the onslaught which left the palace
of the Adhémar a blackened ruin. If there are few spots in
France where one more deeply resents the senseless havoc of
the Revolution, there are few where, on second thoughts,
one so distinctly understands what turned the cannon on the
castle.

The son-in-law of Madame de Sévigné was the most
exorbitant as he was the most distinguished of his race; and it
was in him that the splendour and disaster of the family
culminated. But probably no visions of future retribution
disturbed the charming woman who spent – a victim to her
maternal passion – her last somewhat melancholy years in the
semi-regal isolation of Grignan. No one but La Bruyère seems,

VALENCE: THE CATHEDRAL

in that day, to have noticed the 'swarthy livid animal, crouched over the soil, which he digs and turns with invincible obstinacy, but who, when he rises to his feet, *shows a human countenance*' – certainly he could not be visible, toiling so far below, from that proud terrace of the Adhémar which makes the church its footstool. Least of all would he be perceptible to the eyes – on other lines so discerning! – of the lady whose gaze, when not on her daughter's face, remained passionately fixed on the barrier of northern mountains, and the highway that ran through them to Paris. Paris! Grignan seems far enough from it even now – what an Ultima Thule, a land of social night, it must have been in the days when Madame de Sévigné's heavy travelling carriage had to bump over six hundred miles of rutty road to reach the doors of the Hôtel Carnavalet! One had to suffer Grignan for one's adored daughter's sake – to put up, as best one could, with the clumsy civilities of the provincial nobility, and to console one's self by deliciously ridiculing the pretensions of Aix society – but it was an exile, after all, and the ruined rooms of the castle, and the long circuit of the *chemin de ronde*, are haunted by the wistful figure of the poor lady who, though in autumn she could extol the 'sugary white figs, the Muscats golden as amber, the partridges flavoured with thyme and marjoram, and all the scents of our sachets', yet reached her highest pitch of eloquence when, with stiff fingers and shuddering pen, she pictured the unimaginable February cold, the 'awful beauty of winter', the furious unchained Rhône, and 'the mountains *charming in their excess of horror*'.

Four

THE RHÔNE TO THE SEINE

Fɪ́ʀᴏᴍ Montélimar to Lyons the 'great north road' to
Paris follows almost continuously the east shore of the
Rhône, looking across at the feudal ruins that stud the opposite
cliffs. The swift turns of the river, and the fantastic outline of
these castle-crowned rocks, behind which hang the blue lines
of the Cévennes, compose a foreground suggestive in its wan
colour and abrupt masses of the pictures of Patinier, the
strange Flemish painter whose ghostly calcareous landscapes
are said to have been the first in which scenery was painted
for scenery's sake. In all the subtler elements of beauty, as well
as in the power of historic suggestion, this Rhône landscape far
surpasses that of the Rhine; but, like many of the most beautiful
regions of France, it has a quality of aloofness, of almost classic
reserve, that defends it from the inroads of the throng.

Midway to Lyons, Valence, the capital of Cæsar Borgia's
Valentinois, rises above the river, confronted, on the opposite
shore, by a wild cliff bearing the ruined stronghold of Crussol,
the cradle of the house of Uzès. The compact little Romanesque cathedral of Saint Etienne, scantily adorned by the light
exterior arcade of its nave, is seated on an open terrace
overlooking the Rhône. As sober, but less mellow, within, it
offers – aside from the monument to Pius VI, who ended his
troubled days here – only the comparatively recondite interest
of typical constructive detail; and the impressionist sightseer is
likely to wander out soon to the little square beyond the apse.

Here stands 'Le Pendentif', a curious little vaulted building of the Renaissance, full of the note of character, though its original purpose seems to be the subject of archæological debate. Like many buildings of this part of the Rhône valley, it was unhappily constructed of a stone on which the wear of the weather might suggest the literal action of the 'tooth of Time' – so scarred and gnawed is the whole charming fabric. As to its original use, it appears to have been the mortuary chapel of the noble family whose arms are discernible among the incongruous animals of its decaying sculpture; for it is part of the strangeness of the little monument that the spandrils of its elegant classic order are inhabited by a rude Romanesque fauna which, combined with the dusky hue and ravaged surface of the stone, confers on it, in contrast to the rejuvenated church, a look of mysterious antiquity.

A few yards off, down a dark narrow street, the same savour of the past is found in one of those minor relics which let the observer so much deeper into bygone institutions than the study of their official monuments. This is simply an old private house of the early Renaissance, with a narrow sculptured courtyard, a twisting staircase, and vaulted stone passages and rooms of singularly robust construction. It is still – appropriately enough – inhabited by *une très vieille dame* who has receded so deeply into the farthest convolution of her stout stone shell that her friendly portress had leave to conduct us from basement to attic, giving us glimpses of dusky chambers with meagre venerable furniture, and of kitchens and offices with stone floors, scoured coppers and pots of herbs, all so saturated with the old concentrated life of provincial France that it was like lifting to one's lips a glass of some ancient wine just at the turning-point of its perfection.

Not far from Valence, Tournon springs romantically from a

VIENNE: GENERAL VIEW OF THE TOWN

cliff of the west bank, surmounted by the ducal castle of Soubise; and the next strong impression comes where Vienne, proudest of Rhône towns, lifts its flamboyant cathedral on a vast flight of steps above the river. The site of Vienne, and its long Roman past, prepare one for more interest of detail than a closer inspection reveals. The Roman temple, which may once have rivalled the Maison Carrée, was in the Middle Ages (like the temple of Syracuse) incorporated in a Christian church, and now, extricated lifeless from this fatal embrace, presents itself as an impersonal block of masonry from which all significance of detail is gone. The cathedral, too, has suffered in the same way, though from other causes. In its early days it was savagely mutilated by the Huguenots, and since then the weather, eating deeply into its friable stone, has wrought such havoc with the finery and frippery of the elaborate west front that the exterior attracts attention only as a stately outline.

All the afternoon we had followed the Rhône under a cloudy sky; and as we crossed the river at Vienne the clouds broke, and we pushed northward through a deluge. Our day had been a long one, with its large parenthesis at Grignan, and the rainy twilight soon closed in on us, blotting out the last miles of the approach to Lyons. But even this disappointment had its compensations, for in the darkness we took a wrong turn, coming out on a high suburb of the west bank, with the city outspread below in a wide network of lights against its holy hill of Fourvière. Lyons passes, I believe, for the most prosaic of great French towns; but no one can so think of it who descends on it thus through the night, seeing its majestic bridges link quay to quay, and the double sweep of the river reflecting the million lights of its banks.

*

It was still raining when we continued on our journey the next day; but the clouds broke as we climbed the hill above Lyons, and we had some fine backward glimpses of the Rhône before our road began to traverse the dull plain of the Bresse.

So rest, for ever rest, O princely pair!

If the lines have pursued one from childhood, the easiest – and, alas, the most final! – way of laying their lovely spectre is to turn aside from the road to Dijon and seek out the church of Brou. To do so, one must journey for two or three hours across one of the flat stretches of central France; and the first disillusionment comes when Brou itself is found to be no more than a faubourg of the old capital of the Bresse – the big, busy, cheese-making town of Bourg, sprawling loosely among boundless pastures, and detaining one only by the graceful exterior of its somewhat heterogeneous church.

A straight road runs thence through dusty outskirts to the shrine of Margaret of Austria, and the heart of the sentimentalist sank as we began to travel it. Here, indeed, close to the roadside, stood 'the new pile', looking as new as it may have when, from her white palfrey, the widowed Duchess watched her 'Flemish carvers, Lombard gilders' at work; looking, in fact, as scrubbed, scraped and soaped as if its renovation were a feat daily performed by the 'seven maids with seven mops' on whose purifying powers the walrus so ingeniously speculated. Matthew Arnold's poem does not prepare the reader for the unnatural gloss which makes the unhappy monument look like a celluloid toy. Perhaps when he saw it the cleansing process had not begun – but did he ever really see it? And if so, where did he see the

Savoy mountain meadows,
By the stream below the pines?

And how could he have pictured the Duchess Margaret as being 'in the mountains' while she was supervising the work? Or the 'Alpine peasants' as climbing 'up to pray' at the completed shrine, or the priest ascending to it by the 'mountain-way' from the walled town 'below the pass'?

Is Bourg the walled town, and its dusty faubourg the pass? And shall we, when we pass under the traceries of the central door, and stand beneath the vaulting of the nave, hear overhead the 'wind washing through the mountain pines'? It will have to travel a long way to make itself heard!

Poor Lady Mary Wortley Montagu, so maligned for her imaginative pictures of Lovere and Lake Iseo, may surely be forgiven for having gilded the lily, for adding an extra touch of romance where the romantic already so abounded; but it is less easy to explain how the poet of the church of Brou could evoke out of the dusty plain of the Bresse his pine-woods, streams and mountains. Perhaps (the pilgrim reflects) the explanation will be found within the church, and standing in the magic light of the 'vast western window' we too shall hear the washing of the wind in the pines, and understand why it travelled so far to reach the poet's ear.

In this hope we enter; but only to discover that inside also the archæological mops have been at work, and that the elaborate lining of the shrine is as scoured and shiny as its exterior. Well! let us affront this last disenchantment – and the little additional one of buying a ticket for the choir from a gold-braided custodian at a desk in the nave – and closing our eyes to the secularized, museumized aspect of the monument,

BROU: TOMB OF MARGARET OF AUSTRIA IN THE CHURCH

try to open them to a vision of what it may have been before it was turned into a show.

Alas! even this last effort – this *bon mouvement* of the imagination fails to restore an atmosphere of poetry to the church of Brou, to put it in any other light than that of a kind of superlative 'Albert Memorial', in which regardlessness of cost has frankly predominated over æsthetic considerations. Yet it is manifestly unfair to charge the Duchess Margaret with the indiscrimination of the *parvenu*. One should rather ascribe to special conditions of time and place that stifling confusion of ornament, that air of being, as Bacon puts it, so terribly 'daubed with costs', which is both the first effect and the final outcome of an inspection of Brou. If Arnold gave the rein to fancy in his *mise-en-scène*, he was quite exact in picturing the conditions in which the monument was produced, and his enumeration of the 'Flemish carvers, Lombard gilders, German masons, smiths from Spain' who collaborated in its making, reminds one that artistic unity could hardly result from so random an association of talents. It was characteristic of the time, of the last boiling-over of the heterogeneous Gothic pot, that this strange fellowship was not felt to be any obstacle to the production of a work of art. One sees the same result in almost all the monuments of the period, especially where the Spanish–Netherlands influence has added a last touch of profusion – and confusion. How could an art so evolved issue in anything but a chaos of overdone ornament? How could line survive in such a deluge of detail? The church of Brou is simply the most distressing because the most expensive product of the period. Expiring Gothic changed its outline as often as the dying dolphin is supposed to change his colours – every ornament suggests a convulsion in stone.

And on all this extravagance of design, which could be

redeemed only by the lightest touch of the chisel, lies the heavy hand of the Flemish sculptor. Is it possible that the same phase of artistic feeling produced the three tombs of Brou and those of the Dukes of Burgundy at Dijon? Certainly at least, the same hand did not carve them. At Brou the innumerable subordinate figures – angels, mourners and the rest – are turned out with the unerring facility of the pastry-cook's art: they represent the highest achievement in sugar and white of egg. At Dijon, on the contrary, each *pleureur* in the arcade beneath the tomb of Duke Philip is a living, sentient creature, a mourner whose grief finds individual utterance. Is there anything in plastic art that more vividly expresses the passionate mediæval brooding over death? Each little cowled figure takes his grief, his sense of the *néant*, in his own way. Some are wrung and bowed with it. One prays. Another, a serene young man, walks apart with head bent above his book – the page of a Stoic, one conjectures. And so each, in his few inches of marble, and in the confinement of his cramped little niche, typifies a special aspect of the sense of mortality – above all of its loneliness, the way it must be borne without help.

The thought came to one, the next day at Dijon, the more vividly by contrast to the simpering sorrow of Brou. The tombs of the dukes of Burgundy, so cruelly torn from the hallowed twilight of the Chartreuse, and exposed to the cold illumination of museum windows, give one, even in this impersonal light, a strong sense of personality. Even the overladen detail of the period, the aimless striving of its frets and finials, cannot obscure the serious purity of the central conception; and one is led to the conclusion that a touch of free artistic emotion will break through the strongest armour of stock formulas.

One sees them, of course, the ducal tombs, in a setting in a certain sense their own, since this privileged city, in addition to its other distinctions, has a mediæval palace for its museum, and the mailed heels of the recumbent dukes may have rung on the stone flagging of the Salle des Gardes where they now lie. But the great vaulted hall has ceased to be a guardroom, as they have ceased to be its lords, andd the trail of label and number, of velvet cord and iron rail, is everywhere in their democratized palace. It is noteworthy, therefore, that, as the tombs have retained so much of their commemorative value, so the palace itself has yielded as little as might be of its private character to the encroachments of publicity: appearing almost, as one wanders from one bright room to another, like the house of a great collector who still lives among his treasures.

This felicitous impression is partly due to the beauty of the old building, and partly also to the fact that it houses a number of small collections, the spoils of local dilettanti, each kept together, however diversified its elements, so that many of the rooms exhibit a charming habitable mingling of old furniture, old porcelain and the small unobtrusive pictures that are painted to be lived with, not glanced up at from a catalogue.

The impression of happy coincidences, of really providential accidents, which gives such life to the bright, varied museum, persists and deepens as one passes from it into the town – the astonishing town which seems to sum up in itself almost every phase of French art and history. Even the deep soil of France has hardly another spot where the past grows so thick and so vigorously, where the ancient growths lift such hale heads to the sunlight. The continuity of life at Dijon is as striking as its diversity and its individuality. Old Dijon is not

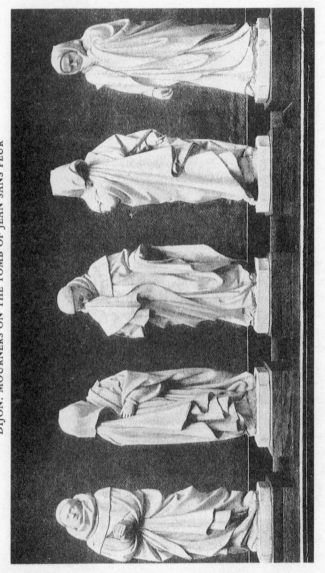

DIJON: MOURNERS ON THE TOMB OF JEAN SANS PEUR

an archipelago of relics in a sea of modern houses: it is like a
vascular system, binding the place together in its network of
warm veins, and seeming, not to be kept alive, but to be
keeping life in the city.

It is to this vivid synthesis of the past that one reverts from
even the strongest single impressions – from the civic sump-
tuousness of the Palais de Justice, the elegance of the Hôtel de
Vogué, the mysterious symbolism of the jutting row of
gargoyles on the west front of Notre Dame – suffering them
to merge themselves, these and many more, into a crowded
splendid tapestry, the mere background of the old city's
continuous drama of ducal, Imperial, parliamentary life.

The same impression of richness, of deep assimilated
experience, accompanies one on the way north through the
Burgundian province – giving to the trivial motorist, the mere
snarer of haphazard impressions, so annihilating a sense of his
inability to render even a superficial account of what he sees,
and *feels beneath the thing seen*, that there comes a moment
when he is tempted to take refuge in reporting the homely
luxury of the inns – though even here the abundance of
matter becomes almost as difficult to deal with.

It is for this reason, perhaps, that after a morning among
the hills and valleys of the Morvan, in sight, almost continuously, of that astonishing Burgundian canal, with its long lines
of symmetrical poplars, its massive masonry, its charming lock-
houses, all repeating themselves like successive states of a
precious etching – that after such a morning I seek, and seem
to find, its culminating astonishment in the luncheon which
crowned it in the grimy dining-room of the *auberge* at Précy-
sous-Thil. But was it an *auberge*, even, and not rather a *gargote*,
this sandy onion-scented 'public', with waggoners and soldiers
grouped cheerfully about their *petit vin bleu*, while a flushed

handmaid, in repeated dashes from the kitchen, laid before us a succession of the most sophisticated dishes – the tenderest filet, the airiest *pommes soufflées*, the plumpest artichokes that ever bloomed on the buffet of a Parisian restaurant? It corresponded, at any rate, to the kind of place where, in any Anglo-Saxon country, one would have found the company as prohibitory as the food, and each equally a reason for fleeing as soon as possible from the other.

So it is that Précy-sous-Thil may stand as a modest symbol of the excessive amenity of this mellowest of French civilizations – the more memorably to one party of hungry travellers because it formed, at the same time, the final stage of their pilgrimage to Vézelay.

That thought, indeed, distracted us from the full enjoyment of the filet, and tore us from the fragrant coffee that our panting waitress carried after us to the motor's edge; for more than half the short April day was over, and we had still two hours of steep hill and vale between ourselves and Vézelay.

The remainder of the way carried us through a region so romantically broken, so studded with sturdy old villages perched on high ledges or lodged in narrow defiles, that but for the expectation before us every mile of the way would have left an individual impression. But on the road to Vézelay what can one see but Vézelay? Nothing, certainly, less challenging to the attention than the loftily seated town of Avallon which, midway of our journey, caught and detained us for a wondrous hour.

The strain of our time limit, and the manifold charms of the old town, so finely planted above the gorge of the Cousin, had nearly caused us to defer Vézelay, and end our day's journey at the Hôtel du Chapeau Rouge. But in the mild air, and on the extreme verge of the bright sky, there was a threat

AVALLON: GENERAL VIEW OF THE TOWN

of rain, and the longing to see the great Benedictine abbey against such a sunset as the afternoon promised was even stronger than the spell of Avallon. We carried away therefore (with the fixed intention of returning) only the general impression of a walled town set against a striking background of cliff and woodland, and one small vivid vignette of a deserted square where aged houses of incredible picturesqueness grouped themselves at scenic angles about the sculptured front of the church of Saint Lazare.

From Avallon to Vézelay the road winds to the west, between the leafy banks of the Cousin, through the town of Pontaubert, with its ancient church of the Templars, past the bridge of the Cure, and out at last into the valley dominated by the conical hill of Vézelay. All day the vision of the Benedictine church had hung before us beyond each bend of the road; and when at length we saw its mighty buttresses and towers clenched in the rock, above the roofs and walls of the abbatial town, we felt the impact of a great sensation – for the reality was nobler than the vision.

The mere sight of Vézelay from the valley – quite apart from the rush of associations it sets free – produces the immediate effect of one of those perfect achievements in which art and nature interpret and fulfil each other. The church stands just where such a building should stand, and looks as a building should look to be worthy of such a site. The landscape about it has the mingled serenity and ruggedness which its own lines express, and its outline grows out of the hill-top without a break between the structural harmony of the two.

Before mounting up to compare the detailed impression with the first effect, one is detained by the village of Saint Père (Pierre) sous Vézelay, which lies just at the foot of the

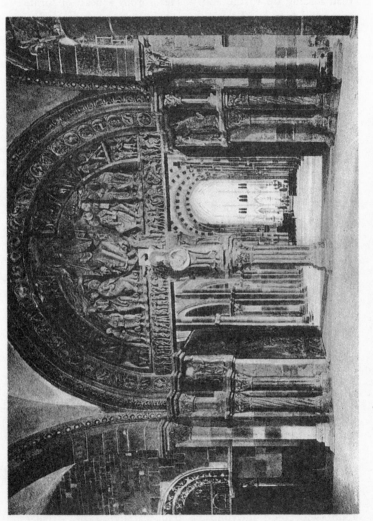

VÉZELAY: NARTHEX OF THE CHURCH OF THE MADELEINE

road leading up to the abbey. Here, from a heap of sordid houses, and among stifling barnyard exhalations, rises the sweet worn old church of Saint Pierre, younger in date than the abbey church above, but stained and seamed by time. From the stone embroideries of its triple porch and its graceful fantastic narthex, it might pass, at first glance, for a more than usually temperate specimen of flamboyant Gothic; but if one backs away far enough to take in its whole outline, the upper façade and the tower reveal themselves as an exquisite instance of thirteenth-century transition. The tower, in particular, with its light ranges or arcades, and the slender trumpeting angels that so surprisingly buttress its angles, seems, as an observant traveller has already noted, more Italian than Burgundian – though to find its match in Italy one would have to seek, not among actual church towers, but in the backgrounds of early Tuscan pictures, where, against a sky of gold leaf, such heralds sound their call from the thatch of the manger.

After the mystical vision of the bell-tower of Saint Père it is almost a drop back to prose to climb the hill to Vézelay and stand before the church of the Magdalen – or rather it is like turning from the raptures of Joachim of Flora or Hugo of Saint Victor to the close-knit dialectic of Saint Thomas Aquinas. This vast creation of mediæval faith might indeed be likened to the great doctrinal system out of which it grew – such a strong, tight, complex structure, so studied, balanced and mathematically exact it seems.

It has seen, the great church, in its well-nigh thousand years of existence, sights so splendid and memorable that it seems at first a mere background for its memories – for the figures of Saint Bernard and Becket, of Philip Augustus and Cœur de Lion, with their interminable train of clerical and secular dignitaries, monks, nobles, doctors of the Church, and all the wild impassioned rout of the second and third Crusades. To have seen so much, and now to stand so far apart from life! One reflects on the happier fate of those other great churches of lay growth, the French cathedrals, whose hearts beat warm for so many centuries, through so many social and political alternations.

The situation of the church of Vézelay typifies this deeper solitude. It stands alone on the crest of the hill, divided from the town below by a wide stony square. Behind the apse, where the monastic buildings lay, a shady grassy slope simulates the privacy of an English close – and on all sides are the blue distances of the Morvan. This loftiness and detachment of site give a peculiar majesty to the building, and conduce no doubt to the impression that in all church architecture there is nothing quite like it, nothing in which the passive strength of the elder style so imperceptibly blends with the springing grace of the new. The latter meets one first, in the two-storeyed narthex, a church in itself, which precedes the magnificent round-arched portals of the inner building. It is from the threshold of this narthex that, looking down its lofty vista, and through the triple doorways to the vast and stern perspective of the Romanesque nave, one gets the keenest impression of the way in which, in this incomparable building, the two styles have been wrought into an accord that shows their essential continuity. In the nave itself, with the doors of the narthex closed, another, subtler impression awaits one; for here one seems to surprise the actual moment of transition, to see, as nowhere else, the *folded wings of the Gothic* stirring under the older forms.

More even than its rich, mysterious sculptures, far more than its mere pride of size and majesty, does this undefinable *fremissement* of the old static Romanesque lines remain with one as the specific note of Vézelay: giving it, in spite of its age-long desertion, in spite of the dead and staring look produced by indiscriminate restoration, an inner thrill of vitality, the promise of 'strange futures beautiful and young', such as the greatest art alone possesses.

The long spring sunset filled the sky when we turned from Vézelay and began to wind through the valley of the Cure to Auxerre. The day had been too rich in impressions to leave space for more than a deep sense of changing loveliness as we followed the curves of the river through poplar-planted meadows, by white chalk-cliffs and villages hanging on the heights. But among these fugitive impressions is the vivid memory of a white railway viaduct, so lightly yet securely flung across the valley that in the golden blur of sunset it suggested one of Turner's dream-bridges spanning a vale of Tempe: a notable instance of the almost invariable art with which, in French engineering, the arch is still employed. After that the way grew indistinct, and night had fallen when we entered Auxerre – feeling our way through a dimly lit suburb, seeing the lights of the town multiplied in the quiet waters of the Yonne, and reaching it at last by a bridge that led straight to the steep central street.

Auxerre, the next day – even through the blinding rain which so punctually confirmed our forebodings – revealed itself as one of those closeknit, individual old French towns that are as expressive, as full of vivacity and character, as certain French faces. Finely massed above the river, in a pile culminating with the towers of the cathedral and the detached shaft of Saint Jean, it confirms, and indeed exceeds, on a nearer view, the promise of its distant aspect. A town which has had the good fortune to preserve its walls and one or two of its fortified gates, has always – and more especially if seated on a river – the more obvious opportunities for picturesqueness; and at Auxerre the narrow streets rising from the quay to the central group of buildings contribute many isolated effects – carved door, steep gable or opportune angle-turret – to the general distinction of the scene.

The cathedral itself is the heart of the charming old place – so rich in tone, so impressive in outline, so profusely yet delicately adorned, it rose at the end of the long market-square, shedding on it, even through the grey sheets of rain, the warmth of its high tawny masses. The design of the western front is so full and harmonious that it effaces from memory the less salient impression of the interior. Under a more favourable light, which would have brought out the colours of the rich clerestory glass, and the modelling of shafts and vaulting, it would have seemed, no doubt, less austere, more familiarly beautiful; but veiled and darkened by rain-clouds it offered, instead of colour and detail, only an unfolding of cavernous arches fading into the deep shades of the sanctuary.

The adjoining Bishop's palace, with its rugged Romanesque arcades planted on a bit of Gallo-Roman city wall, and the interesting fragment of the church of Saint Germain, beside the hospital, are among the other notable monuments of Auxerre; but these too, masked by the incessant downpour, remained in memory as mere vague masses of dripping masonry, pressed upon by a low black sky.

The rain pursued us northward from Auxerre along the valley of the Yonne, lifting a little toward noon to leave the landscape under that grey-green blur through which the French *paysagistes* have most persistently seen it. Joigny, with this light at its softest, seemed, even after Auxerre, one of the most individual of ancient French towns: its long and stately quay, closed by a fine gate at each end of the town, giving it in especial a quite personal character, and one which presented itself as a singularly happy solution of the problem of linking a town to its river. Above the quay the steep streets gave many glimpses of mediæval picturesqueness, tucked away at almost inaccessible angles; but the rain closed in on them, and drove us on reluctantly to Sens.

Here the deluge hung a still denser curtain between us and the amenities of this singularly charming town. Sens, instead of being, like Joigny, packed tight between river and cliff, spreads out with relative amplitude between Roman ramparts transformed into shady promenades; and about midway of the town, at the end of a long market-place like that of Auxerre, the cathedral rears itself in such nobility and strength of line that one instantly revises one's classification of the great French churches to make room for this one near the top.

Its beauties develop and multiply on a nearer view, and its kinship with Canterbury makes it, to those under the spell of that noblest of English choirs, of peculiar architectural interest. But when one has done full justice to the long unfolding of the nave, to the delicate pallor of Cousin's glass, and to the associations attached to the 'altar of Becket' behind the choir, one returns finally to the external composition of the apsidal chapels as the most memorable and perfect thing at Sens. The development of the *chevet*, which Romanesque architecture bequeathed to Gothic, is perhaps the happiest product of the latter growth on French soil; and after studying so complex an example of its possibilities as the apse of Sens presents, one feels anew what English Gothic lost in committing itself to the square east end.

Of great historic interest is the so-called *Officialité* which adjoins the cathedral – a kind of diocesan tribunal built under Louis IX; but its pointed windows and floriated niches have been so liberally restored that it has the too Gothic look of a mediæval stage-setting. Sens has many other treasures, not only in its unusually rich collection of church relics and tapestries, but among the fragments of architecture distributed through its streets; and in the eighteenth-century gates of the archiepiscopal palace it can show a specimen of wrought-iron work probably not to be matched short of Jean Lamour's gates at Nancy.

One of its most coveted possessions – Jean Cousin's famous picture of the *Eva prima Pandora* – has long been jealously secluded by its present owner; and one wonders for what motive the inveterate French hospitality to lovers of art has been here so churlishly reversed. The curious mystical interest of the work, and its value as a link in the history of French painting, make it, one may say, almost a *monument historique*, a part of the national heritage; and perhaps the very sense of its potential service to art gives a perverse savour to its possessor's peculiar mode of enjoying it.

From Sens to Fontainebleau the road follows the valley of the Yonne through a tranquil landscape with level meadows and knots of slender trees along the river, till the border of the forest is reached, and a long green alley takes one straight to the granite cross on the edge of the town. Toward afternoon the rain turned to a quiet drizzle, of the kind that becomes the soft French landscape as a glass becomes certain pictures; and through it we glided on, past the mossy walls of great estates, past low-lying châteaux, green *pièces d'eau*, and the long grassy vistas that are cut in every direction through the forests about Melun. This district of big 'shootings' and carefully tended

SENS: APSE OF THE CATHEDRAL

preserves extends almost to the outer ring of environs. Beyond them Paris itself soon rose smokily through the rain, and a succession of long straight avenues, as carefully planted as if they had been the main arteries of a fashionable suburb, led us thence to the Porte de Choisy.

To be back in the roar of traffic, to feel the terrific pressure of those miles of converging masonry, gave us, after weeks of free air and unbounded landscape, a sense of congestion that made the crowded streets seem lowering and dangerous; but as we neared the river, and saw before us the curves of the lifted domes, the grey strength of the bridges, and all the amazing symmetry and elegance of what in other cities is mean and huddled and confused, the touch of another beauty fell on us – the spell of '*les seuils sacrés, la Seine qui coule*'.

PART THREE

A FLIGHT TO THE NORTH-EAST

THERE ARE SEVERAL ways of leaving Paris by motor without touching even the fringe of what, were it like other cities, would be called its slums. Going, for instance, southward or south-westward, one may emerge from the alleys of the Bois near the Pont de Suresnes and, crossing the river, pass through the park of Saint Cloud to Versailles, or through the suburbs of Rueil and Le Vésinet to the forest of Saint Germain.

These miraculous escapes from the toils of a great city give one a clearer impression of the breadth with which it is planned, and of the civic order and elegance pervading its whole system; yet for that very reason there is perhaps more interest in a slow progress through one of the great industrial quarters such as must be crossed to reach the country lying to the north-east of Paris.

To start on a bright spring morning from the Place du Palais Bourbon, and follow the tide of traffic along the quays of the left bank, passing the splendid masses of the Louvre and Notre Dame, the Conciergerie and the Sainte Chapelle; to skirt the blossoming borders of the Jardin des Plantes, and cross the Seine at the Pont d'Austerlitz, getting a long glimpse down its silver reaches till they divide to envelop the Cité; and then to enter by the Boulevard Diderot on the long stretch of the Avenue Daumesnil, which leads straight to the Porte Dorée of Vincennes – to follow this route at the leisurely pace necessitated by the dense flow of traffic, is to get a memorable idea of the large way in which Paris deals with some of her municipal problems.

The Avenue Daumesnil, in particular, with its interminable warehouses and cheap shops and *guinguettes*, would anywhere else be the prey of grime and sordidness. Instead, it is spacious, clean, and prosaic only by contrast to the elegance of the thoroughfares preceding it; and at the Porte Dorée it gives one over to the charming alleys of a park as well tended and far more beautiful than the Bois de Boulogne – a park offering the luxury of its romantic lawns and lakes for the sole delectation of the packed industrial quarters that surround it.

The woods of this wonderful Bois de Vincennes are real woods, full of bluebells and lilies of the valley; and as one flies through them in the freshness of the May morning, Paris seems already far behind, a mere fading streak of factory smoke on the horizon. One loses all thought of it when, beyond Vincennes, the road crosses the Marne at Joinville-sur-Pont. Thence it passes through a succession of bright semi-suburban villages, with glimpses, here and there, of low white châteaux or of little grey churches behind rows of clipped hornbeam; climbing at length into an open hilly country, through which it follows the windings of the Marne to Meaux.

Bossuet's diocesan seat is a town of somewhat dull exterior, with a Gothic cathedral which has suffered cruelly at the hands of the reformers; for, by an odd turn of fate, before becoming the eyrie of the 'Eagle', it was one of the principal centres of Huguenot activity – an activity deplorably commemorated in the ravaged exterior of the church.

From Meaux to Rheims the country grows in charm, with a slightly English quality in its rolling spaces and rounded clumps of trees; but nothing could be more un-English than the grey-white villages, than the stony squares bordered by clipped hornbeams, the granite market-crosses, the round-apsed churches with their pointed bell-towers.

One of these villages, Braisne, stands out in memory by virtue of its very unusual church. This tall narrow structure, with its curious western front, so oddly buttressed and taper-ing, and rising alone and fragmentary among the orchards and kitchen gardens of a silent shrunken hamlet, is the pathetic survival of a powerful abbey, once dominating its surround-ings, but now existing only as the parish church of the knot of sleepy houses about it.

A stranger and less explicable vestige of the past is found not far off in the curious walled village of Bazoches, which, though lying in the plain, must have been a small feudal domain, since it still shows its stout mediæval defences and half-fallen gate-towers tufted with wall-flowers and wild shrubs. The distinguishing fact about Bazoches is that it is not a dwindled town, with desert spaces between the walls and a surviving nucleus of houses: its girdle of stone fits as closely as a finger-ring, and whatever were its past glories they must have been contained in the same small compass that suffices it today.

Beyond Braisne the country is less hilly, the pastures are replaced by vineyards, and the road runs across a wide plain to Rheims. The extent of the town, and its modern manufactur-ing outskirts, make its distant silhouette less characteristic than that of Bourges or Chartres, which are still so subordinated to the central mass of their cathedrals. At Rheims the cathedral comes on one unexpectedly, in the centre of the town; but once seen it enters into the imagination, less startlingly but perhaps more completely, more pervasively, than any other of the great Gothic monuments of France. This sense of being possessed by it, subdued to it, is perhaps partly due – at least in the case of the simple tourist – to the happy, the unparalleled fact, that the inn at Rheims stands immediately opposite the cathedral – so that, admitted at once to full communion with its incomparable west front, one returns, after each excursion, to renew and deepen the relation, to become reabsorbed in it without any conscious effort of attention.

There are two ways of feeling those arts – such as sculpture, painting and architecture – which appeal first to the eye: the technical, and what must perhaps be called the sentimental way. The specialist does not recognize the validity of the latter criterion, and derision is always busy with the uncritical judgements of those who have ventured to interpret in terms of another art the great plastic achievements. The man, in short, who measures the beauty of a cathedral not by its structural detail consciously analysed, but by its total effect in indirectly stimulating his sensations, in setting up a movement of associated ideas, is classed – and who shall say unjustly? – as no better than the reader who should pretend to rejoice in the music of Lycidas without understanding the meaning of its words. There is hardly a way of controverting the axiom that thought and its formulation are indivisible, or the deduction that, therefore, the only critic capable of appreciating the beauty of a great work of architecture is he who can resolve it into its component parts, understand the relation they bear to each other, and not only reconstruct them mentally, but conceive of them in a different relation, and visualize the total result of such modifications.

Assuredly – yet in those arts that lie between the bounds of thought and sense, and leaning distinctly toward the latter, is there not room for another, a lesser yet legitimate order of appreciation – for the kind of confused atavistic enjoyment that is made up of historical association, of a sense of mass and harmony, of the relation of the building to the sky above it, to the light and shadows it creates about it – deeper than all, of a blind sense in the blood of its old racial power, the things it meant to far-off minds of which ours are the oft-dissolved and reconstituted fragments? Such enjoyment, to be of any value even to the mind that feels it, must be based indeed on an approximate acquaintance with the conditions producing the building, the structural theories that led up to it, their meaning, their evolution, their relation to the moral and mental growth of the builders – indeed, it may be affirmed that this amount of familiarity with the past is necessary to any genuine æsthetic enjoyment. But even this leaves the enjoyment under the slur of being merely 'amateurish', and therefore in need of a somewhat courageous defence by those who, unequipped for technical verdicts, have yet found a more than transient satisfaction in impressions of this mixed and nebulous order.

Such a defence is furnished, to a degree elsewhere unmatched, by the exceptional closeness of intercourse to which propinquity admits the traveller at Rheims. Here is the great Presence on one's threshold – in one's window: surprised at dawn in the mystery of its rebirth from darkness; contemplated at midday in the distinctness of its accumulated detail, its complex ritual of stone; absorbed into the mind, into the heart, again at darkness – felt lastly and most deeply under the midnight sky, as a mystery of harmony and order no less secret and majestic than the curves of the stars in their orbits.

Such pleasures, at any rate, whatever their value as contributions to special lines of knowledge, enrich the æsthetic consciousness, prepare it for fresh and perhaps more definite impressions, enlarge its sense of the underlying relation

between art and life, between all the manifold and contradictory expressions of human energy, and leave it thus more
prepared to defend its own attitude, to see how, in one sense
– a sense not excluding, but in a way enveloping and fertilizing
all the specialized forms of technical competence – *Gefühl ist
alles.*

It is one of the wonders of this rich north-eastern district that
the traveller may pass, in a few hours, and through a region
full of minor interest, to another great manifestation of
mediæval strength: the fortress of Coucy. Two such contrasting specimens of the vigour – individual and collective – of
that tremendous age are hardly elsewhere, in France, to be
found in such close neighbourhood; and it adds to the interest
of both to know that Coucy was a fief of Rheims, bestowed
by its Archbishop on a knight who had distinguished himself
in the First Crusade. It was a great-grandson of this Enguerrand
de Boves who built the central keep and the walls; but the
castle was further enlarged and adorned when, at the beginning
of the fifteenth century, it passed into the possession of Louis
d'Orléans, the brother of Charles VI.

It is doubly interesting to see Coucy after Carcassonne,
because the two fortresses present the opposite extremes of
feudal secular architecture, Carcassonne being the chief surviving example of a large walled town with a comparatively small
central castle, while at Coucy the castle is the predominating
feature, both in size and site, and the town no more than a
handful of houses within the outer circuit of its defences. Both
strongholds are, of course, situated on steep heights, and that
of Coucy, though it rises from slopes clad in foliage, and
therefore less stern of outline than the dry southern rock of

Carcassonne, stands no less superbly than its rival. In fact there is perhaps no single point from which Carcassonne produces quite such an effect of concentrated power as the keep and castle towers of Coucy squaring themselves on their western ridge. Yet such comparisons are unprofitable, because the two fortresses were designed for purposes so different, and under such different conditions, that the one is necessarily most vigorous where the other had the least need for a display of strength.

Coucy, in its present fallen state, gains incalculably from the charm of its surroundings – the lovely country enfolding it in woods and streams, the shaded walks beneath its ivy-hung ramparts, and above all the distinct and exquisite physiognomy of the tiny old town which these ramparts enclose. The contrast between the humble yet stout old stone houses ranged, as it were, below the salt, and the castle throned on its dais of rock at one end of the enclosure, seems to sum up the whole social system of the Middle Ages as luminously and concisely as Taine's famous category. Coucy has the extraordinary archæological value of a place that has never outgrown the special institutions producing it: the hands of the clock have stopped at the most characteristic moment of its existence; and so impressive, even to the unhistorical mind, is its compact and vivid 'exteriorization' of a great phase of history, that one wonders and shudders at, and finally almost comes to admire, the superhuman stolidity of the successful merchant who has planted, on the same ledge as the castle, and almost parallel with its Titanic towers, a neatly turreted suburban villa, the sole attempt of modern Coucy to give the retort to its overwhelming past.

*

Taking Coucy as a centre, the traveller may, within a few hours, extraordinarily vary his impressions, since the remarkable group of monuments distributed over the triangular bit of France between Paris, Rheims and Saint Quentin comprises a characteristic example of almost every architectural period from the early Middle Ages till the close of the eighteenth century – the extremes being sometimes in as close touch as Tracy-le-Val and Prémontré.

Turning first to the west, through a country of rolling fields and wooded heights, vaguely English in its freedom from the devouring agriculture of the centre, one comes on the most English impression in France – the towers of Noyon rising above a girdle of orchards and meadows. Noyon, indeed, to the end, maintains in one this illusion – so softly misted with verdure, so lacking in the sharp edges of the dry stony French town, it seems, by its old street-architecture of cross-beams and stucco, by the smoothly turfed setting of the cathedral, and the crowning surprise of a genuine 'close' at its back, to corroborate at every step the explorer's first impression.

In the cathedral, indeed, one is no longer in England – though still without being very definitely in France. For the interior of Noyon, built at a time when northern art was still groping for its specific expression, is a thing apart in cathedral architecture, one of those fortunate variations from which, in the world of art as of nature, new forms are sometimes developed. That in this case the variation remained sterile, while it makes, no doubt, for a more exclusive enjoyment of Noyon, leaves one conjecturing on the failure to transmit itself of so original and successful an experiment. The deviation consists, principally, in the fact that the transept ends of Noyon are rounded, so that they form, in conjunction with the choir, a kind of apsidal trefoil of the most studied and consummate

ST QUENTIN: HÔTEL DE VILLE

examples of both; and how the men triumph and stand out, how Rousseau and d'Alembert, Maurice de Saxe and the matchless Vernezobre overshadow and efface all the Camargos and Dauphinesses, the Favarts and Pompadours of the varied feminine assortment! Only one little ghostly nameless creature – a model, a dancer, the catalogue uncertainly conjectures – detaches herself from the polite assemblage as if impaled with quivering wings on the sharp pencil of the portraitist. One wonders if she knew she had been caught . . .

The short run from Saint Quentin to Laon carries one, through charming scenery, from the Low Countries into a region distinctively French, but with such a touch of romance as Turner saw in the sober French landscape when he did his 'Rivers and Harbours'. Laon, the great cathedral town of the north-east, is not seated on a river; but the ridge that carries it rises so abruptly from the plain, and so simulates the enclosing curves of a bay, that, as we approached it, the silvery light on the spring fields at its base seemed like the shimmer of water.

Seen from the road to Saint Quentin, Laon is one of the stateliest hill-towns of France – indeed it suggests rivalry with the high-perched Umbrian cities rather than with any nearer neighbours. At one extremity of the strangely hooked cliff, the two ends of which bend toward each other like a thumb and forefinger, stands the ruined abbey church of Saint Vincent, now a part of the arsenal; at the other rises the citadel, behind which are grouped the cathedral and episcopal palace; and the apex of the triangle, between these pronged extremities, is occupied by the church of Saint Martin, which lifts its Romanesque towers above the remains of a Premonstratensian abbey. In the sheltered hollow enclosed between the thumb and forefinger lies the *Cuve de Saint Vincent*, a garden district of extraordinary fertility, and beyond it the interminable plain flows away toward the Belgian frontier.

To the advantage of this site Laon adds the possession of well-preserved ramparts, of two or three fortified gates to which clusters of old houses have ingeniously attached themselves, and above all of its seven-towered cathedral – a cathedral now no longer, though its apse still adjoins an ancient group of diocesan buildings, from the cloistered court of which one obtains the finest impression of the lateral mass of the monument.

Notre Dame of Laon ranks in size among the 'secondary' French cathedrals; but both in composition and in detail it occupies a place in architecture as distinctive as its natural setting, and perhaps no higher praise can be awarded it than to say that, like the church of Vézelay, it is worthy of the site it occupies.

The seven towers of Laon are its most notable ornament; no other cathedral roof of France bears such a glorious crown. Four only of the towers have received their upper tiers of arcades; but the others rise high enough above the roof-ridge to break its outline with their massive buttresses and pyramidal capping. The taller four are distinguished by the originality of their upper storeys, of which the intermediate one is octagonal, and broken up into four groups of arches of extreme lightness and vigour, separated by stilted round-arched openings which are carried through to the upper tier of the tower. At the west end of the church, the open niches formed by the octagonal sally of the tower-arcades are filled by colossal stone oxen, modelled with a bold realism, and advancing from their high-perched stalls almost as triumphantly as the brazen horses above the door of Saint Mark's.

LAON: GENERAL VIEW OF THE TOWN AND CATHEDRAL

These effigies are supposed to commemorate the services of the patient beasts who dragged the stone for the cathedral up the cruel hill of Laon; and looking up at their silhouettes, projected ponderously against the blue, one is inclined to see in them a symbol of mediæval church building − of the moral and material cost at which Christianity reared its monuments.

The oxen of Laon and the angels of Saint Père sous Vézelay might indeed be said to stand for the two chief factors in this unparalleled outburst of religious activity − the visionary passion that aroused it, and the painful expenditure of human and animal labour that made the vision a reality. When one reads of the rapidity with which many of these prodigious works were executed, of the fever of devotion that flamed in whole communities, one has, under the gladness and exalta-tion, glimpses of a drudgery as unceasing and inconceivable as that of the pyramid-builders, and out of which, perhaps, have grown the more vigorous, the stabler fibres of European character − and one feels that the triumphing oxen of Laon, though they stand for so vast a sum of dull, unrewarded, unintelligible toil, have on the whole done more for civiliza-tion than the angels of Saint Père.

At Soissons, an old city saturated with Roman and Merovin-gian memories, Gothic art again triumphs, but in a different and a milder strain.

The short run from Laon to Soissons, through a gently undulating landscape, prepares one for these softer impressions. The Gallo-Roman city has neither the proud site nor the defensive outline of Laon. It lies in the valley of the Aisne, in a circle of wooded hills, with the river winding peaceably between the old town and its faubourg of Saint Vaast. Passing through this faubourg, and crossing the Aisne, one is caught in a maze of narrow streets, which lead up tortuously to the cathedral square. The pressure of surrounding houses makes it difficult to get a comprehensive view of the church, but one receives, in narrow glimpses through the clipped limes of the market-place, a general impression of grace and sobriety that somehow precludes any strong individual effect. The cathedral of Soissons is indeed chiefly remarkable for its repetition of the rounded transepts of Noyon; though in this case (for reasons which it would be interesting to learn) the round end, while receiving the further development of an aisle and triforium, has been applied only to one transept.

The thought of Soissons, however, at least in the mind of the passing impressionist, must remain chiefly associated with that rarest creation of the late Gothic of the north-east, the façade of Saint Jean des Vignes. This church, which formed part of a monastic settlement in the outskirts of the town, is now almost in ruins, and of the abbatial buildings around it there remain only two admirable fragments of the cloister arcade, and the abbot's house, built at a much later date. So complete is the outline of the beautiful west front that one would hardly guess the ruin of the nave but for the blue sky showing through the vast circle of the central rose, from which every fragment of tracery has been stripped. Yet one can pardon even that inhumanity to the destroyers who respected the towers – those incomparable towers, so harmonious in their divergences, so typical of that lost secret of mediæval art – the preservation of symmetry in unlikeness. These western towers of Saint Jean, rising strongly on each side of the central door, and reinforcing the airy elegance of the façade by their vigorous vertical buttressing, break, at the level of the upper gable, into pyramidal masses of differing

SOISSONS: RUINED CHURCH OF SAINT–JEAN–DES–VIGNES

height and breadth, one more boldly tapering, the other more massive and complex, yet preserving in a few essential features – the placing of the openings, the correspondence of strong horizontal lines – a unity that dominates their differcnces and binds them into harmony with the whole façade. It is sad, on passing through the gaping western doorway, to find one's self on a bit of waste ground strewn with fragments of sculpture and masonry – sadder still to have the desolation emphasized by coming here on a bit of Gothic cloister, there on a still more distinctive specimen of Renaissance arcading. The quality of these surviving fragments indicates how great must have been the interest, both æsthetic and historical, of this beautiful ruin, and revives the vain wish that, in some remote corner of Europe, invasion and civil war might have spared at least one complete example of a great monastic colony, enabling one to visualize the humaner side of that mediæval life which Carcassonne evokes in its militant aspect.

The return from Soissons to Paris holds out so many delightful alternatives, in respect both of scenery and architecture, that, in April especially, the traveller may be excused for wavering between Compiègne and Senlis, between Beauvais and Saint Leu d'Esserent. Perhaps the road which traverses Senlis and Saint Leu, just because it offers less exceptional impressions, brings one closer to the heart of old France, to its inexhaustible store of sober and familiar beauty. Senlis, for instance, is only a small sleepy town, with two or three churches of minor interest – with that the guide-book might dismiss it; but had there been anything in all our wanderings quite comparable to the impression produced by that little cathedral in its quiet square – a monument so compact yet noble, so embroidered with delicate detail, above all so sunned-over with a wonderful golden lichen that it seems like a dim old jewel-casket from which the gilding is almost worn?

The other churches of Senlis, enclosed, like the cathedral, in the circuit of half-ruined walls that make a miniature *cité* of the inner town, have something of the exquisite quality of its central monument. Both, as it happens, have been secularized, and Saint Pierre, the later and more ornate of the two buildings, has suffered the irony of being converted into a market, while Saint Frambourg, an ancient collegiate church, has sunk to the uses of a storage warehouse. In each case, access to the interior is sometimes hard to obtain; but the two façades, one so delicate in its early Gothic reticence, the other so prodigal of the last graces of the style, carry on almost unbrokenly the architectural chronicle which begins with the Romanesque cathedral; and the neglect, so painful to witness in the interior, has given them a surface-tone almost rich enough to atone for the cost at which it has been acquired.

If, on leaving Senlis, one turns westward, skirting the wooded glades of Chantilly, and crossing the park at the foot of the 'Canal de la Manche', one comes presently into the valley of the Oise and, a few miles further on, the village of Saint Leu d'Esserent lifts its terraced church above the river.

The site of Saint Leu is that of the little peaked Mediterranean towns: there is something defensive, defiant, in the way it grasps its hill-side and lifts its church up like a shield. The town owes this crowning ornament – and doubtless also its own slender existence – to the founding here, in the eleventh century, of a great Cluniac abbey, of which certain

Romanesque arcades and a fortified gate may be traced among the debris behind the apse. Of the original church there survives only a round-arched tower, to which, in the latter half of the twelfth century, was added what is perhaps the most homogeneous, and assuredly the most beautiful, early Gothic structure in France. The peculiar interest of this church of Saint Leu – apart from its intrinsic nobility of design – lies in the fact of its being, so curiously, the counterpart, the other side of the shield, of the church of Vézelay. For, as at Vézelay one felt beneath the weight of the round openings the impatient stirrings of the pointed arch, so here at Saint Leu, where the latter form at last triumphs, its soaring movement is still held down by the close-knit Romanesque frame of the church. It is hard to define the cause of this impression, since at Saint Leu the pointed style has quite freed itself, structurally, from Romanesque *entraves*, all the chief elements of later Gothic construction being blent there in so harmonious a composition that, as Mr Charles Moore has pointed out, the church might stand for a perfect example of 'unadorned Gothic'. All that later art could do toward the elaboration of such a style was to add ornament, enlarge openings, and lighten the masses. But by the doing of just that, the immense static value of the earlier proportions was lost – and the distinction of Saint Leu is that it blends, in perfect measure, Gothic lightness with Romanesque tenacity.

Of this the inside of the church is no less illustrative than its exterior. Though the western bays of the nave were built later than its eastern portion, they end in a narthex on the lines of the outer porch of Vézelay, surmounted by a gallery from which the great sweep of the aisles and triforium may be felt in all its grandeur. For, despite the moderate proportions of the church, grandeur and reserve are its dominating qualities

– within and without it has attained the classic balance that great art at all times has its own ways of reaching.

Westward from Saint Leu, the valley of the Oise, fruitful but somewhat shadeless, winds on toward Paris through pleasant riverside towns – Beaumont, l'Isle-Adam, and the ancient city of Pontoise; and beyond the latter, at a point where the river flings a large loop to the west, one may turn east again and, crossing the forest of Saint Germain, descend on Paris through the long shadows of the park of Saint Cloud.